Nādabindu Upaniṣad
Dhyānabindu Upaniṣad

Meditations on the Inner Sound

Original Sanskrit text with
Transliteration, Translation and Commentary

Commentary by
Swāmī Satyadharma Saraswatī

Translation and Transliteration by
Śrimukti (Ruth Perini)

Dedication

To all friends, practitioners

and teachers of yoga,

and to all seekers of spiritual wisdom,

regardless of time or place, creed,

gender, age or race

CONTENTS

page

Foreword 1
Introduction 4
Nādabindu Upaniṣad
Invocation 11
Verse
1. Symbol of Aum 14
2. Quality of Aum 16
3-4. Origin of the seven lokas 18
5-6a. Power of Mantra 20
6b-7. Three letters of Aum 22
8. Oṃkāra 24
9-11. Twelve Śaktis of Oṃkāra 25
12. Passing during the first mātrā 28
13. During the second, third or fourth 30
14. During the fifth 31
15. During the sixth, seventh or eighth 32
16. During the ninth, tenth, eleventh or twelfth 33
17. Śiva and Aum 34
18. Entry into Śiva consciousness 36
19. Important advice regarding meditation 38
20. Freedom from worldly duties 40
21. Acceptance of prārabdha 42
22-23a. Tattwajñāna and prārabdha 44
23b-24a. Prārabdha and rebirth 46
24b-25a. What is the source of illusion? 47
25b-26a. Where is the universe? 48
26b-27. The snake and the rope 49
28-29a. Purpose of prārabdha 51
29b-30. Self-realisation 53
31. Nāda yoga 55
32. Inner sound 57
33-35. Sounds heard in nāda yoga 59
36. Sound of the drum 61
37-38. Focusing on one sound 62
39. Absorption into space 64
40. Sound meditation 65
41. Absorption in sound 66
42-43a. Quality of absorption 67
43b-44a. One-pointed concentration on nāda 68

44b-46a. Nāda restrains the mind 69
46b-47a. Praṇava nāda 71
47b-48a. Space and sound 72
48b-51a. Beyond the mind 73
51b-53. Direct path to liberation 76
54-56. Signs of liberation 78
Appendices
1. Pronunciation Guide 82
2. Sanskrit Text 84
3. Continuous Translation 91
Dhyānabindu Upaniṣad
Invocation 98
Verse
1. Dhyāna yoga destroys sin 100
2. Bindu nāda 102
3. Highest stage of nāda yoga 103
4. Power of the supreme nāda 104
5-7. Knowledge of Brahman 105
8. Self is both manifest and unmanifest 108
9a. Meditation on Om 110
9b-13a. Three components of Om 111
13b-15. Qualities of a Brahman 113
16-19. The power of Oṃkāra 114
20-25. Oṃkāra meditation 116
26-29. Lotus of the heart 119
30-35. Meditating on Viṣṇu Brahma and Śiva 121
36-37. Knowledge of the Vedas 124
38-40. Abode of the Supreme Spirit 125
41. Six limbs of yoga 127
42-43a. Main postures 128
43b-50a. First three cakras 129
50b-53. Nāḍīs 132
54-58a. Nāḍīs and prāṇa 134
58b-61a. Jīva 136
61b-65a. Mantra Haṃsa Haṃsa 138
65b-68. Parameśvarī 140
69. Raising Prāṇa 142
70. Doors of the Nāḍīs 143
71-73. Awakening Kuṇḍalinī 144
74-75a. Mūlabandha 146
75b-77. Uḍḍiyāna Bandha 147

78-79a. Jālandhara Bandha 148
79b-82a. Results of Khecarī Mudrā 149
82b-86a. Khecarī Mudrā 151
86b-91a. Two kinds of bindu 153
91b-93. Mahā Mudrā 155
94. The Ātman 157
95-97a. Meditating on the bīja mantras of the five elements 165
97b-99a. One jīva 167
99b-105. Praṇava 168
Appendices
1. Sanskrit text 172
2. Continuous translation 185
About the Author 197
About the Translator 198

Foreword

Swami Satyadharma Saraswati, 1946 - 2019

On 12th June 2019 on the Central Coast of New South Wales, Australia, our beloved Swami Satyadharma left her body. It was on the day of Ganga Dussehra, celebrating the descent to Earth of the goddess Ganga, Ganga the mother providing nourishment to all her children.

Dedications in the Yoga Upanishad books have been to all spiritual aspirants. Swami Satyadharma's life was dedicated for over forty years to providing spiritual nourishment and bringing the light of yoga to all those who attended her programs throughout the world.

Swami Satyadharma was born to a middle-class family in Connecticut, USA. She was the youngest of three and lived surrounded by nature and animals. She recognised the spiritual energy of nature, and was never attracted to big cities.

In search of purpose and spiritual guidance she travelled for years throughout Europe, Africa and Asia, where she met many enlightened masters. When taking part in a meditation program in Java, Indonesia in the mid 1970's, she was directed by the master to go to Mungher, Bihar, India, where she would meet a great teacher, Swami Satyananda, a disciple of Swami Sivananda. There she stayed for thirty-five years.

At the age of 28, she was initiated by Swami Satyananda into *pūrṇa sannyasa* (full renunciation), a Dashnami order connected with the Advaita Vedanta tradition established by Adi Shankaracharya to protect, preserve and propagate spiritual knowledge. She absorbed the teachings and worked hard for the ashram for the first twenty years she spent there.

Then she edited books written by Swami Satyananda and, under his guidance, travelled the world teaching a range of different spiritual courses on the Yogic Scriptures. And teach she did in Australia, USA, Canada, India, Nepal, Tibet, China, Japan, Korea, Columbia, Greece, Germany, Hungary, France, Italy, Indonesia, New Zealand. In all those countries she was invited to come back time and time again. She had a great ability to teach. Her vast knowledge of the ancient scriptures was amazing. It just flowed from her. When she taught it was like she stepped into another zone, where she spoke with profound insight. That is why, if Swami Satyadharma was running a course, people would sign up regardless of the topic. Her deep understanding of yoga was reflected in the numerous topics she taught.

Her later years were devoted to writing commentaries on the Yoga Upanishads. She had completed her commentary on Nādabindu, and had written her commentary on only nine verses of Dhyānabindu. No-one else has completed this commentary, or been asked to do so, as her commentaries were original and unique.

Swami Satyadharma's Programs, Retreats and Lectures

Programs
Awakening Kundalini, Meditations from the Tantras, Dancing with Divine, Atma Darshan, Intuition, Guru Tattwa, Shiva Sutras, Mantra Yantra and Mandala, Ashram Life, Sadhana, Chakra Meditation, Spiritual Life.

***Deepening Sadhana* Retreats**
Kriya Yoga, Tattwa Shuddhi, Chakra Shuddhi, Prana Vidya

and Mahavidya Sadhana.

Lectures

During the years she lived in Australia, she gave many satsangs and lectures to students enrolled in Yogic Studies courses. Topics included Origins of Yoga, Samkhya Tantra & Vedanta, Yoga Sutras, Koshas, Chakras, Gunas, Bhagavad Gita, SWAN Theory, Raja Yoga, Gyan Yoga, Bhakti Yoga, Karma Yoga, Hatha Yoga, Upanishads, Pranava, Shiva Shakti, Mantra & Nada, Mantra Yoga, Nada Yoga, Mudra & Bandha, Shatkarmas, Kundalini Yoga, Swara Yoga, Prana & Pranayama, Pratyahara, Theory & Practice of Antar Mouna, Yoga Psychology, Yoga Philosophy, Yoga in India, Yoga Ecology, Yoga History, Path of the Rishis, Yamas & Niyamas, Yoga & Religion, Meditation, Yoga Nidra, Addiction, Purpose in Life, Grief, Body-Mind Therapy, Opening the Heart, Perception, Models of Mind, Mind & Consciousness, Mind Management and Living Consciously.

We were privileged to have worked with Swami Satyadharma for many years. We know her unlimited love and teachings will live on well beyond our lifetimes.

Om Tat Sat

Introduction

Veda is a Sanskrit word meaning 'knowledge'. In the context of the Vedas, it means 'revealed knowledge which is *śruti*, 'heard' from within, not taught. These ancient spiritual texts or hymns, through which we can learn much of the perceptions and insights of the early vedic seers, are grouped into four *samhitas* or collections: *Rig Veda, Yajur Veda, Sāma Veda* and *Atharva Veda*. They were revealed to enlightened beings 3,000 to 4,500 years ago or more (the Rig-Veda contains astronomical references describing occurrences in 5,000 to 3,000 BCE), and transmitted orally by the sages from generation to generation within brahmin families.

The four Vedas were considered to be divine revelations, and each word was carefully memorised. This was to ensure accurate transmission, but also because each syllable was considered to have spiritual power, its source being the supreme, eternal sound. This was a mammoth task, as there are 20,358 verses in the four Vedas, approximately two thousand printed pages. They were composed in fifteen different metres, which demanded perfect control of the breath. Georg Feuerstein describes them as 'a composite of symbol, metaphor, allegory, myth and story, as well as paradox and riddle' and their composers as 'recipients and revealers of the invisible order of the cosmos [with] inspired insights or illumined visions'1.

Rig Veda

The Rig Veda is the oldest spiritual text in the world and still regarded as sacred, containing 1,028 hymns or songs of 10,589 verses in praise of the divine (*rig* or *ric* meaning 'praise'). Each hymn is recognised as a *mantra*, a sacred sound vibration, which releases energy from limited material awareness, thus expanding the consciousness. It is also the earliest surviving form of Sanskrit. The illumined seers composed the hymns while established in the highest consciousness, thus able to commune with luminous beings of the higher realms. There are about 250 hymns in praise of *Indra*, the divine force behind the ocean, heavens, thunder, lightning, rain and the light of the sun; 200 of *Agni*, born of the Sun, becoming the god of sacrificial fire, and over 100 of *Soma*, who gives immortality, and who is connected to the Sun, Moon, mountains, rivers and oceans. Others are dedicated to *Varuna*, who protects cosmic order; the *Ashvins*, supreme healers; *Ushas*, goddess of the dawn; *Aditi*, goddess of eternity; and *Saraswati*, goddess of the Vedas and of music and the arts.

Yajur Veda

The hymns of the Yajur-Veda, Veda of Sacrifice, consist of sacrificial formulas or prayers, including those of an internal or spiritual nature, which are chanted by the *adhvaryu* (priest), who performs the sacrifice. About a third of its 1,975 verses are taken from the Rig Veda. The rest are original and in prose form.

Sāma Veda

The Sāma Veda, Veda of Chants, gives instructions on the chanting of vedic hymns. The majority of its 1,875 verses are from the Rig Veda; only 75 verses are original. Many of the hymns were sung by special priests during sacrificial rites. Some are still sung today.

Atharva Veda

The Atharva Veda, named after the seer Atharvan, whose family were great seers in vedic times, contains 731 hymns of 5,977 verses, about one fifth of which are from the RigVeda. Much of the Atharva Veda consists of magical spells and charms for gaining health, love, peace and prosperity, or taking revenge on an enemy. Possibly for this reason, the Atharva Veda was either not accepted by the orthodox priesthood, or not given the same standing as the other Vedas.

The vedic people and their culture

The vedic people lived for over 2,500 years mainly along the banks of the Saraswati River, which was located in Northern India between the modern Ravi and Yamuna Rivers down to what is now the desert of Rajasthan. The Saraswati River dried up in about 1,900 BCE due to tectonic upheavals. Other areas of habitation included the Ganges River and its tributaries, rivers in Afghanistan (previously called Gandhara), the Himalayas and Mount Kailash in Tibet.

The vedic people had a complex multi-tiered view of the universe, in which humankind, nature and the divine are intertwined and interrelated. They had a deep knowledge of the oceans, mountains, deserts and forests of the physical world, as well as of the subtle worlds of deities and different levels of consciousness. People lived in cities or villages or were nomads, and were fully engaged in worldly life. They were an agrarian people, yet also had herds of cattle, horses and camels. Cities were constructed of stone, bricks and metal. They built chariots and ships. They were skilled workers in gold, metal, clay, stone, wood, leather and wool, and showed a very high standard in arts, crafts, astrology, medicine, music, dance and poetry.

After the Vedas

The Vedas were the foundation for the later revelations (*śruti*) in the *Brāhmaṇas* (ritual texts), the *Āranyakas* (texts on rituals and meditation for forest-dwelling ascetics) and the *Upaniṣads* (esoteric texts). Later still, the Vedas were the basis for numerous works of remembered or traditional knowledge, known as *smṛti,* including the epics: i.e. the *Mahābhārata, Rāmāyaṇa* and *Purāṇas,* and the *Sūtras,* or threads of knowledge, e.g. *Yoga Sūtras.* All these texts contain many concepts and practices, which come directly from the four Vedas.

Upaniṣads

The word *upaniṣad* is comprised of three roots: *upa* or 'near', *ni* or 'attentively', and *sad,* 'to sit'. The term describes the situation in which these unique texts were transmitted. The students or disciples sat near the realized master and listened attentively, as he expounded his experiences and understanding of the ultimate reality. These teachings are said to destroy the ignorance or illusion of the spiritual aspirant in regard to what is self and non-self, what is real and unreal, in relation to the absolute and relative reality. Only disciples were chosen, who had persevered in *sādhana catuṣṭaya*, the four kinds of spiritual effort, viz. *viveka* (discrimination between the permanent and impermanent), *vairagya* (non-attachment), *ṣadsampatti* (six virtues of serenity, self-control, withdrawal of the senses, endurance, perfect concentration and strong faith) and *mumukṣutva* (intense desire for liberation).

The Upaniṣads are derived from the Āranyakas, because they were chanted in the forest (*āranya*) after the aspirant had retired from worldly life. They are recorded in the later form of Sanskrit used in the Brāhmaṇas, and considered the last phase of *śruti*, vedic revelation. The Upaniṣads are regarded as *vedānta*, the end of the Vedas, inferring that *vedānta* is the end or completion of all perceivable knowledge, as they guide the aspirant beyond the limited mind to the *ātman* (spiritual self) and thus to *mokṣa* (liberation). Each upaniṣad reflected the teachings and tradition of a realized master, and was connected with a specific Veda and vedic school. It is estimated that there are over 200 Upaniṣads, which have been divided into seven groups: *Major*, *Vedānta*, *Śaiva*, *Śakta*, *Vaiśnava*, *Sannyasa* and *Yoga.*

Yoga Upaniṣads

The twenty one Yoga Upaniṣads give an understanding of the hidden forces in nature and human beings, and describe esoteric yogic practices by which these forces can be manipulated and controlled. They emphasise that the inner journey to the one permanent reality, the *ātman*, is the essential one. Journeys to external places, such as holy sites and temples, as well as rituals and ceremonies, are not given importance. Their teachings give important information on the subtle body (*cakras, koṣas, prāṇa, kuṇḍalinī,* meditative states), and the tantric and yogic techniques, not given in the earlier upaniṣads, to attain them. Therefore, they are regarded as a significant integration of Vedanta and Tantra, which were previously considered incompatible. They are classified as 'minor' only because they postdate Ādi Śaṅkara.

Although their teachings actually predate Patañjali, the Yoga Upaniṣads were codified after the *Yoga Sūtras of Patañjali,* and form an important part of the classical yoga literature. However, they contain no references to Patañjali or his *Yoga Sūtras*. So, although the compilation of the Yoga Upaniṣads is post-Patañjali, the *vidyās*, or meditative disciplines, contained within them are pre-Patañjali. The Yoga Upaniṣads emerged at a time when the vedic and tantric cultures were coming together to share their knowledge. The wise thinkers from each culture sat down together and discussed how their insights and teachings could be combined in order to benefit humanity. Thus these upanisads combine the teachings of both tantra and yoga. It is evident in them that yoga leads to vedānta, and vedānta leads to yoga. However, they were written down by vedantic scholars and practitioners in order to show that these *vidyās* and related practices were not borrowed from Patañjali, but were known and practised from the ancient period.

Within the twenty-one Yoga Upaniṣads are six sub-groups which have their own main focus. The *Bindu Upaniṣads*, which include the *Amṛta-Bindu* (also known as the *Brahma-*

Bindu-Upaniṣad), *Amṛta-Nada-Bindu*, *Nada-Bindu*, *Dhyāna-Bindu* and *Tejo-Bindu-Upaniṣads*, all concentrate on the bindu, the source or origin of all sound, and hence of creation. Bindu represents the transcendental sound manifested in the mantra *Aum*. The *Hamsa-Mantra*, *Soham*, is the main practice of the *Hamsa*, *Brahma-Vidya*, *Mahavakya* and *Paśupata-Brahma-Upaniṣads*. Concentration on *prāṇa*, the life force related to the process of inhalation and exhalation, brings the yogin to the knowledge of the transcendental self. The light of pure consciousness, which the enlightened irradiate is the theme of the *Advaya-Taraka* and *Maṅḍala-Brahmana-Upaniṣads*. The *Kṣurika-Upaniṣad* (*kṣurika* meaning 'dagger') emphasises non-attachment as a means to liberation. The sixth group, comprised of eight late Yoga Upaniṣads from 1200 to 1300 A.D., covers teachings related to hatha and kundalini yogas. They are the *Yoga-Kuṅḍalī*, *Yoga-Tattwa*, *Yoga-Śikhā*, *Varāha*, *Śāndilya*, *Tri-Śikhi-Brahmana*, *Yoga-Darśana* and *Yoga-Cūdāmani Upaniṣads*.

The Dhyāna and Nādabindu Upaniṣads were probably composed between the ninth and fourteenth centuries CE. The bindu is a psychic centre located in the brain at the top back of the head. These upaniṣads focus on meditation on the bindu, the source point or origin of individual creation, where begins the primal sound or first vibration, the mantra Om. They define and describe in detail the mantra Om, the effects of meditating on it until one attains perfect liberation, merging with the Divine.

Nādabindu describes the components of Om, that is, its three and a half measures (*mātrā*) which are the sounds *a u m*, and the half measure, the echo of *m*. Always meditating on Om, the yogin is liberated from worldly life, unaffected by his/her karmas. The nāda is first heard through the right ear, and many other inner sounds are heard. Eventually the yogin hears no other sounds and transcends duality.

Dhyānabindu, an expansion of Nādabindu, confirms that meditation on Om can destroy all karmas. The yogin should meditate on the lotus of the heart, then at the eyebrow centre, then on the Sun, Moon and Agni, leading to the ātman. The six parts of yoga, the cakras, nāḍīs and prāṇas are described. Kuṇḍalinī Śakti can be awakened by the repetition of the mantra *haṃsa*, *ham* spontaneously accompanying the inhalation, and *sa* the exhalation, as well as uḍḍiyāna and jālandhara bandhas, khecarī mudrā and mahāmudrā. The ātman is described in detail. Finally, the teacher recommends meditating on the bija mantras of the five elements, the five prāṇas and the nāda. Swami Satyadharma completed her commentary on Nādabindu, and passed away while writing the commentary on Dhyānabindu.

References

Saraswati, Swami Satyadharma. *Yoga Chudamani Upanishad* (Yoga Publications Trust, Munger, Bihar, India, 2003)

Aiyar, N.K. *Thirty Minor Upanishads* (Parimal Publications, Delhi, India 2009)

Feuerstein, Georg and Kak, Subhash and Frawley, David. *In Search of the Cradle of Civilization* (Quest Books, Illinois, USA 2001)

1. *ibidem* p.20

Feuerstein, Georg. *The Yoga Tradition* (Hohm Press, Prescott, Arizona USA 2001

Frawley, David. *Gods, Sages and Kings* (Passage Press, Salt Lake City, Utah USA 1991)

नादबिन्दूपनिषत्

nādabindūpaniṣat

Sound-Point Upaniṣad

Opening Invocation

वैराजात्मोपासानाया संजातज्ञानवह्निना ।
दग्ध्वा कर्मत्रयं योगी यत्पदं याति तद्भजे ।।
ॐ बाङ्मे मनसीति शान्तिः ।।

vairājātmopāsanaya saṃjātajñānavahninā
dagdhvā karmatrayaṃ yogī yatpadaṃ yāti tadbhaje
om vānme manasīti śāntiḥ

Anvay

dagdhvā: having burned; *karma-trayam*: three *karmas*; *vahninā*: through the fire; *jñāna*: knowledge; *saṃjāta*: born; *upāsanaya*: through devotion to; *ātma*: self; *vairājāt*: derived from Virāj (Brahma); *yogī*: yogin, adept in yoga; *yāti*: goes to; *yat padam*: that seat; *tat bhaje*: where he worships; *om*: Om, cosmic primal soumd; *iti*: let there be; *śāntiḥ*: peace; *manasi*: in mind; *vānme*: in speech.

Translation

Having burned the three *karmas* through the fire of knowledge, born through devotion to the self, [who is] derived from Virāj, the yogin goes to that seat where he worships.

Om, let there be peace in speech and mind.

Commentary

The three karmas referred to at the beginning of the text

relate with our mental conditioning and nature, which are formed by the impressions stored in the memory from our actions. These include our current actions, as well as the past actions that accrue over many lifetimes. The impressions of all our actions, past and present, are stored in the subconscious field, or *citta*, and are known as *sancita karmas*. They form our individual associations and memories, which are a unique and indelible blue print of our person. The current actions, which we are in the process of performing from moment to moment, are called *kriyamana* or *agami* karmas. These karmas are likened to the arrow, which has been placed in the bow, aimed and drawn back, but is not yet released. So, there is still some element of self-determination, freewill or choice. One may yet decide whether or not to release the arrow, or to perform the action. The accumulated actions, which have ripened and are ready to be expressed, are called *prārabdha*, or destined, karmas. They are unchangeable, and must simply be enjoyed or endured, when their time comes.

Karma is the basis of human bondage. Every action we perform is stored in the consciousness in the form of an impression, or *samskara*. Hence the words samskara and karma are often used interchangeably. No action or karma is ever lost, disappears or goes away. All the karmas are there in their store, even though we may forget about them, or think they are gone. The ultimate goal of all yogas and all sādhanas is to attain liberation from the bondage of karma.
Therefore, the yogin, who has burned through these three karmas by the fire of *brahma jñāna*, knowledge of the transcendental consciousness, born through devotion to the self, goes to the seat of worship. In this sense, worship is not a state of prayer or praise, but a deep and abiding affinity with the divine source of all existence. Keeping this aim in mind, the rishi, or revealer of the upaniṣad says, "Om, let

there be peace in speech and mind," for this is the condition necessary to confer this teaching on nāda bindu from master to student.

Verse 1: Symbol of Aum

ॐ अकारो दक्षिण: पक्ष उकारस्तूत्तरः समृतः ।
मकारं पुच्छमित्याहुरर्धमात्रा तु मस्तकम् ।।१।।
om akāro dakṣinaḥ pakṣa ukārastūttaraḥ smṛtaḥ
makāraṃ pucchamityāhurardhamātrā tu mastakam (1)

Anvay

akāraḥ: sound 'a'; *smṛtaḥ*: is declared; *dakṣiṇaḥ pakṣaḥ*: right wing; *om*: AUM, sound of Brahma; *ukāraḥ*: sound 'u'; *uttaraḥ*: left; *makāram*: sound 'm'; *puccham*: tail; *ardhamātrā*: half-syllable; *āhuḥ*: is said; *mastakam*: head.

Translation

The sound 'a' is declared [to be] the right wing [of] AUM, 'u' the left, 'm' the tail, and the half-syllable is said [to be] the head.

Commentary

The teachings given herein on *nāda bindu* begin with a description of the symbol for the sound *Aum.* This is the primal nāda, or subtlest sound vibration, which ushers the pure consciousness that is unmanifest into the manifest dimension of creation. Meditation on this symbol represents the merging of nāda and bindu, the primal point from which all form evolves, at the source, or the beginning of evolution. Nāda bindu is the exact point of transition, when creation begins to unfold from its source, the pure consciousness, and then again, when the manifest creation dissolves back into the unmanifest source.

Therefore, in relation to nāda bindu, there are two ways to meditate upon Aum. The first way is through the path of nāda, hearing the sound or repeating the sound. The second way is the path of bindu, whereby the practitioner focuses on the form or symbol. In this verse the second way is given precedence. The symbol or form of Aum is described here in relation to its three letters: A, U and M, which form the symbol in the Sanskrit or Devanagari script.

Verse 2: Quality of Aum

पादादिकं गुणास्तस्या शरीरं सत्त्वमुच्यते ।
धर्मो ऽस्य दक्षिणं चक्षुरधर्मो ऽथो परः समृतः ।।२।।
pādādikaṃ guṇāstasya śarīraṃ sattvamucyate
dharmo 'sya dakṣiṇaṃ cakṣuradharmo 'tho paraḥ smṛtaḥ (2)

Anvay

ucyate: it is said; *guṇāḥ*: *guṇas*, qualities of nature, *tamas, rajas* and *sattvam*; *ādikam*: start at; *pāda*: feet; *tasya śarīram*: its body; *dharmaḥ*: *dharma*, harmony; *smṛtaḥ*: it is declared; *asya dakṣiṇam cakṣuḥ*: its right eye; *athaḥ*: and; *adharma*: *adharma,* disharmony; *paraḥ*: other.

Translation

It is said the *guṇas* start at the feet, *sattvam* is its body; *dharma*, it is declared, is its right eye, and *adharma* its other [eye].

Commentary

The symbol of *Aum*, as described previously, represents the essence of the sound and, therefore, contains within it the potentiality of the entire creation, both manifest and unmanifest. So, it is said that the *guṇas*, or qualities of nature, start at its feet or base, where they remain in equilibrium. The three guṇas are *tamas*: stability, *rajas*: movement, and *sattwa*: balance. Creation begins when there is some slight movement, some slight interaction between the guṇas, causing one of them to become dominant. And so, sattwa becomes dominant as the body of Aum. This signifies that Aum comes into being as a pure and balanced vibration. Whatever becomes manifest enters the dimension of duality. Hence, dharma is its right eye and adharma, its left eye. The eyes here represent the sense of perception. Dharma refers to right perception, which leads to connection and harmony with the divine. Adharma refers to wrong perception, leading to disconnection and disharmony.

Verses 3 and 4: Origin of the seven lokas

भूर्लोकः पादयोस्तस्य भूवर्लोकस्तु जानुनि ।
सुवर्लोकः कटीदेशे नाभिदेशे महर्जगत् ।।३।।
जनोलोकस्तु हृद्देशे कण्ठे लोकस्तपस्ततः ।
भ्रुवोर्ललाटमध्ये तु सत्यलोको व्यवस्थितः ।।४।।

bhūrlokaḥ pādayostasya bhūvarlokastu jānuni
suvarlokaḥ kaṭideśe nābhideśe maharjagat (3)
janolokastu hṛddeśe kaṇṭhe lokastapastataḥ
bhruvorlalātamadhye tu satyaloko vyavasthitaḥ (4)

Anvay

bhūrlokaḥ: *bhūrloka*, first plane of consciousness; *tasya pādayoḥ*: in its feet; *bhūvarlokaḥ*: *bhūvarloka*, second plane of consciousness; *jānuni*: in [its] knees; *suvarlokaḥ*: *suvarloka*, third plane of consciousness; *deśe*: in the region; *kaṭī*: hips; *mahaḥ-jagat*: *maharjagat*, fourth plane of consciousness; *deśe*: in the region; *nābhi*: navel; *janaḥ-lokaḥ*: *janoloka*, fifth plane of consciousness; *vyavasthitaḥ*: is located; *deśe*: in the region; *hṛd*: heart; *tataḥ*: from there; *lokaḥ-tapaḥ*: *tapoloka*, sixth plane of consciousness; *tu*: and; *satya-lokaḥ*: *satyaloka*, seventh plane of consciousness; *madhye*: in the centre; *lalāta*: forehead; *bhruvoḥ*: eyebrows.

Translation

The *bhūrloka* [is] in its feet, the *bhūvarloka* in its knees; *suvarloka* in the region [of] the hips; *maharjagat* in the region [of] the navel. *Janoloka* is located in the region [of] the heart; from there *tapoloka* in the throat, and *satyaloka* in the centre [of] the forehead [between] the eyebrows.

Commentary

Here *Aum*, being the first vibration of creation, is described as containing the *lokas*, or planes of existence, within it. Again, the form or symbol of *Aum* is used as a foundation to place the seven planes. The *bhūrloka*, or earth plane, lies at its feet, or base. *Bhūvarloka*, the intermediary or spacial plane, is in its knees. *Suvarloka*, the heavenly plane, is in the hip region. *Mahaloka*, the great plane beyond heaven, is in the navel region. *Janoloka*, the plane where pure-minded souls dwell, is located in the heart region. *Tapoloka*, the plane where great yogis and tapasvis dwell, is located in the throat. And *Satyaloka*, the plane of absolute truth, is at the centre of the forehead, in-between the eyebrows.

Verses 5 and 6a: Power of mantra

सहस्रार्णमतीवात्र मन्त्र एष प्रदर्शितः ।

एवमेतं समारूधो हंसयोगविचक्षणः ॥५॥

न भिद्यते कर्मचारैः पापकोटिशतैरपि ।६।

sahasrārṇamatīvātra mantra eṣa pradarśitaḥ
evametaṃ samārūdho haṃsayogavicakṣaṇaḥ (5)
na bhidyate karmacāraiḥ pāpakoṭiśatairapi. (6a)

Anvay

eṣa: flowing; *pradarśitaḥ*: is explained; *atra*: here; *iva*: as; *sahasra-arṇa*: thousand-waved; *mati*: intelligence; *vicakṣaṇaḥ*: one who is proficient; *samārūdhaḥ*: having mounted; *evam*: thus; *haṃsa*: *haṃsa*, able to distinguish between reality and impermanence; *na bhidyate*: is not affected; *karma-caraiḥ*: by the bonds of *karma*, fruits of action; *api*: or even; *śataiḥ*: by a hundred; *koṭi*: crores; *pāpa*: sins.

Translation

The flowing *mantra* is explained here as a thousand-waved intelligence. One who is proficient [in] *yoga*, having thus mounted the *haṃsa*, is not affected by the bonds of *karma* or even by a hundred crores [of] sins.

Commentary

Mantra is an ancient science, which developed very early in human civilization. The word mantra comes from two roots: *manan*, meaning 'mind', and *trayati*, 'liberates'. *Mananāt trayati iti mantra:* that which liberates the mind is mantra. When mantra is repeated or utilised for meditation on a regular basis, it creates a vibratory field that imbues the mind and consciousness with the power of that specific sound vibration, as well as harmony and clarity. Here mantra is described as a thousand waves of flowing intelligence. When you add that kind of dose to the ordinary mind, it becomes extraordinary.

Today, we consider an extraordinary mind to be one capable of regurgitating many facts and figures, or accomplish various feats in the external world. However, in the spiritual context, it means one who is able to access the higher plane of mind and consciousness. The major practice of meditation which is given in yoga is mantra. Hence, to be proficient in yoga means to be proficient in mantra. In this verse, the word *haṃsa* has a double meaning. First, haṃsa is a 'swan', which represents the quality of *viveka*, or 'discrimination', because it has the ability to sift milk from water through its beak. Discrimination is not a quality of the ordinary mind, and that is why so few people have it. It is a quality of the higher mind, and is therefore considered to be a yogic quality.

Secondly, *haṃsa* is one of the foremost mantras, along with Aum, contained in the upanishadic texts. These two mantras were practised assiduously by the yogis of old, who attained *samadhi* and self-realisation through them. The mantra *haṃsa* is also practised in reverse, as *Soham*. Haṃsa has two roots: *ham* or 'I', and *saḥ*, 'that'; I am That. The verse states that one, who is proficient in yoga, has mounted the haṃsa, the swan of discrimination. It also refers to the yogi, who has mastered the *haṃsa* mantra, 'I am That (supreme consciousness)', and no longer limits or identifies himself with the individual roles and associations of worldly life. Such a yogi remains unaffected by the bondage of karma, and even by a hundred million sins.

Verses 6b and 7: Three letters of Aum

आग्नेयी प्रथमा मात्रा वायव्येषा तथापरा ।।६।।
भानुमण्डलसंकाशा भवेन्मात्रा तथोत्तरा ।
परमा चार्धमात्रा या वारुणीं तां विदुर्बुधाः ।।७।।

āgneyī prathamā mātrā vāyavyeṣā tathāparā (6b)
bhānumaṇḍalasaṃkāśā bhavenmātrā tathottarā
paramā cārdhamātrā yā vāruṇīṃ tāṃ vidurbudhāḥ (7)

Anvay

prathamā mātrā: first *mātrā*, unit of sound; *āgneyī*: relates to Agni; *eṣā*: second (*lit* that); *vāyavī*: relates to Vāyu; *tathā*: then; *parā*: next; *bhavet*: is; *saṃkāśā*: bright; *maṇḍala*: orb; *bhānu*: sun; *ca*: and; *uttarā*: last; *paramā*: supreme; *ardhamātrā*: half syllable; *tām*: this; *yā viduḥ*: the wise; *budhāḥ*: know; *vāruṇīm*: relates to Vāruṇa.

Translation

The first *mātrā* relates to Agni, the second to Vāyu; then the next is bright [like] the orb [of] the sun, and the last [is] the supreme *ardhamātrā*; this the wise know relates to Vāruṇa.

Commentary

The mantra *Aum* is comprised of three mātrās, syllables or letters, plus a half mātrā. The first syllable is the sound 'A', which relates with *Agni*, lord of fire. The second relates with *Vāyu*, lord of the air or wind. The third relates with *Sūrya*, lord of the sun. The half syllable at the end relates with Vāruṇa, lord of the water, or the sea. In this way, the syllables of *Aum* produce the vibration of the elements necessary for creation: (i) fire, which brings forth transformation, (ii) air, which contains gaseous substance,

(iii) sun, which gives light and heat, and water, the sustainer of life.

Verse 8: Oṃkāra

कालत्रये ऽपि यस्येमा मात्रा नूनं प्रतिष्ठताः ।
एष ओंकार आख्यातो धारणाभिर्निबोधत ।।८।।

kālatraye 'pi yasyemā mātrā nūnaṃ pratiṣṭhatāḥ
eṣa oṃkāra ākhyāto dhāraṇābhirnibodhata (8)

Anvay

nūnam: now; *yasya*: of each; *api*: also; *pratiṣṭhatāḥ*: are formed of; *kālatraye*: three parts; *eṣa ākhyātaḥ*: this is called; *oṃkāraḥ*: *oṃkāra*, sound of AUM; *nibodhata*: you can know; *dhāraṇābhiḥ*: through the *dhāraṇās*, concentration on each part.

Translation

Now the *mātrās* of each are also formed of three parts. This is called the *oṃkāra.* You can know [it] through the *dhāraṇās.*

Commentary

Each mātrā also consists of three parts, and altogether these are called *oṃkāra.* He who or That which names the symbol of Aum is known as oṃkāra. This term is often used as a reference to Shiva or Brahman, in relation to the supreme consciousness from which Aum has arisen. Oṃkāra can only be experienced through meditation. The *dhāraṇās* are practices of meditation, which involve one-pointed concentration. When performed on a regular basis, they strengthen the inner awareness, allowing the practitioner to transcend the mind. This takes the consciousness to a very high level. The dhāraṇās were developed by the yogis and rishis of old, who practised them in the solitude of mountains and forests. They are found in the different upaniṣads.

Verses 9 to 11: Twelve śaktis of Oṃkāra

घोषिणी प्रथमा मात्रा विद्या मात्रा तथापरा ।
पतङ्गिनी तृतीया स्याच्चतुर्थी वायुवेगिनी ।।९।।
पञ्चमी नामधेया तु षष्टी चैन्द्रीयभिधीयते ।
सप्तमी वैष्णवी नाम अष्टमी शांकरीति च ।।१०।।
नवमी महती नाम धृतिस्तु दशमी मता ।
एकादशी भवेन्नारी ब्राह्मी तु द्वादशी परा ।।११।।

ghoṣiṇī prathamā mātrā vidyā mātrā tathāparā
pataṅginī tṛtīyā syāccaturthī vāyuveginī (9)
pañcamī nāmadheyā tu ṣaṣṭī caindrīyabhidhīyate
saptamī vaiṣṇavī nāma aṣṭamī śāṃkarīti ca (10)
navamī mahatī nāma dhṛtistu daśamī matā
ekādaśī bhavennārī brāhmī tu dvādaśī parā (11)

Anvay

prathamā: first; *mātrā*: mātrā, metre; *syāt*: is; *ghoṣiṇī*: Ghoṣiṇī; *tathā*: then; *parā*: next; *vidyā*: Vidyā; *tṛtīyā*: third; *pataṅginī*: Pataṅginī; *caturthī*: fourth; *vāyuveginī*: *Vāyuveginī*; *pañcamī*: fifth; *nāmadheyā*: Nāmadheyā; *ca*: and; *ṣaṣṭī*: sixth; *abhidhīyate*: is called; *aindrī*: Śiva (coming from Indra); *saptamī*: seventh; *vaiṣṇavī*: relates to Viṣṇu; *aṣṭamī*: eighth; *nāma*: name; *śāṃkarī*: Śāṃkarī, relates to Śiva; *navamī*: ninth; *mahatī*: Mahatī; *daśamī*: tenth; *matā*: is regarded as; *dhṛti*: Dhṛti; *ekādaśī*: eleventh; *bhavet*: is; *nārī*: Nārī; *tu*: then; *dvādaśī*: twelfth; *parā brāhmī*: Supreme Reality.

Translation

The first is Ghoṣiṇī, then the next Vidyā, the third Pataṅginī, the fourth Vāyuveginī, the fifth Nāmadheyā; and the sixth is called Śiva, the seventh Vaiṣṇavī, the eighth's name is said [to be] Śāṃkarī, the ninth Mahatī, the tenth is regarded as

Dhṛti, the eleventh is Nārī, then the twelfth [is] the Supreme Reality.

Commentary

In ancient times people deified the forces of nature and experienced their presence behind all aspects of creation. We can say that the deities were the symbolic forms of the natural forces. They were considered to be luminous and divine, and to dwell on higher planes of consciousness. The people worshipped and made offerings to these deities, feeling them to be supporting and blessing their lives on earth. In order to develop a closer relationship and identity with these forces, they gave them names and anthropomorphous forms. Twelve of these divinities are represented here within the three and a half syllables of *Aum.* They are given feminine names and forms, as their role in creation is aligned with Śakti, the energy that brings forth and sustains all beings. Meditation on these forms and qualities is a form of oṃkāra dhāraṇa.

The first śakti is *Ghoṣiṇī*, who gives *prajña*, intuitive wisdom. The second is *Vidyā*, who secures entrance into the plane of the *yakṣas*, pre-vedic divinities, associated with wealth and fertility. The third is *Pataṅginī*, who confers the power to move through the air, like a bird. The fourth is *Vāyuveginī*, who gives the power of very rapid movement. The fifth is *Nāmadheyā*, who confers entry to *Pitṛloka*, the plane of ancestors. The sixth is *Aindri,* or *Indrani,* śakti of Indra, who represents the power of beauty and attraction. The seventh is *Vaiṣnavī*, ṣakti of Viṣṇu, who protects and preserves. The eighth is *Śāṃkarī*, śakti of Śankara, who is benevolent and auspicious. The ninth is *Mahatī*, who is highly esteemed, and bestows greatness and honour. The tenth is *Dhṛti*, who is steadfast and resolute, and bestows firmness, constancy and support. The eleventh is *Nārī*, who gives access to the plane of sādhus and munis. The twelfth is Parabrahmi, śakti of Parabrahman, who confers entry into the supreme reality.

Verse 12: Passing during the first mātrā

प्रथमायां तु मात्रायां यदि प्राणैर्वियुज्यते ।
भरते वर्षराजासौ सार्वभौमः प्रजायते ।।१२।।

prathamāyāṃ tu mātrāyāṃ yadi prāṇairviyujyate
bharate varṣarājāsau sārvabhaumaḥ prajāyate (12)

Anvay

tu: now; *yadi*: if; *prāṇaiḥ-viyujyate*: one is separated from the *prāṇas*, dies; *prathamāyām mātrāyām*: in the first *mātrā*; *jāsau prajāyate*: he is reborn; *sārvabhaumaḥ*: universal monarch; *bharate varṣarā*: in *Bharatavarṣa,* India.

Translation

Now, if he is separated from the *prāṇas* (i.e. dies) in the first *mātrā,* he is reborn [as] a universal monarch in *Bharatavarṣa* (India).

Commentary

Oṃkāra is a lifelong sādhana. In vedic times it was the main practice performed by yogis and rishis during meditation, as well as throughout the day, during any activity. When practised lifelong, in this way, the vibration of Aum permeates one's entire existence. The mantra continues on with every breath and heart beat, and even through the night in dream or deep sleep. *Prāṇa* is the life-force. When the prāṇa departs from the body, that person passes away. Death is imminent for all, who are born in this world. So, it is natural to wonder, where one will go, when the soul passes out of the body. Here and in the following verses, this question is answered for those who live in attunement with the Oṃkāra. If the prāṇa separates from the body, while the first mātrā is repeated, that yogi will be reborn as a universal monarch in *Bharatvarṣa*, which is the ancient name for subcontinent of India.

Verse 13: During the second, third or fourth

द्वितीयायां समुत्क्रान्तो भवेद्यक्षो महात्मवान् ।
विद्याधरस्तृतीयायां गान्धर्वस्तु चतुर्थिका ॥१३॥

dvitīyāyāṃ samutkrānto bhavedyakṣo mahātmavān
vidyādharastṛtīyāyām gāndharvastu caturthikā (13)

Anvay

samutkrāntaḥ: having passed away; *dvitīyāyām*: in the second; *bhavet*: he becomes; *mahātmavān*: great; *yakṣaḥ*: *yakṣa*, supernatural being; *tṛtīyāyām*: in the third; *vidyādharaḥ*: *vidyādhara*, all-knowing supernatural being; *caturthikā*: fourth; *gāndharvaḥ*: *gāndharva*, celestial musician.

Translation

Having passed away in the second, he becomes a great *yakṣa*; in the third a *vidyādhara*; and in the fourth a *gāndharva.*

Commentary

If the yogi passes away during the second syllable, he becomes a great *yakṣa,* with incomparable wealth. Yakṣas are the guardian spirits of hidden natural treasures, found in the earth, trees and pools. If he passes away in the third, he becomes a *vidyādhara*, spirit beings possessed of scientific and esoteric knowledge. If he passes during the fourth, he becomes a *gāndharva*, celestial musician.

Verse 14: During the fifth

पन्त्रम्यामथ मात्रायां यदि प्राणैर्वियुज्यते ।
उषितः सह देवत्वं सोमलोके महीयते ।।१४।।

pañcamyāmatha mātrāyāṃ yadi prāṇairviyujyate
uṣitaḥ saha devatvaṃ somaloke mahīyate (14)

Anvay

atha: then; *yadi*: if; *prāṇaiḥ-viyujyate*: he is separated from the *prāṇas*, dies; *pañcamyām*: in the fifth; *uṣitaḥ*: he lives; *soma-loke*: in the world of the moon; *saha*: as; *mahīyate*: exalted; *devatvam*: as a *deva*, divine being.

Translation

Then, if he is separated from the prāṇas in the fifth, he lives in the world [of] the moon as exalted as a *deva.*

Commentary

If he passes during the fifth, he will live in the world of the moon, as exalted as a god. The moon was considered to be the storehouse of *soma*, the elixir of immortality. Soma elevates the consciousness, and only the gods could partake of it.

Verse 15: During the sixth, seventh or eighth

षष्ठ्यामिन्द्रस्य सायुज्यं सप्तम्यां वैष्णवं पदम् ।
अष्टम्यां व्रज्यते रुद्रं पशूनां च पतिं तथा ।।१५।।

ṣaṣṭhyāmindrasya sāyujyaṃ saptamyāṃ vaiṣṇavaṃ padam
aṣṭamyāṃ vrajyate rudraṃ paśūnāṃ ca patiṃ tathā (15)

Anvay

ṣaṣṭhyām: in the sixth; *sāyujyam*: communion; *indrasya*: with Indra; *saptamyām*: in the seventh; *vrajyate*: he reaches; *padam*: seat; *vaiṣṇavam*: of Viṣṇu; *ca tathā*: and then; *aṣṭamyām*: in the eighth; *rudram*: Rudra; *patim*: lord; *paśūnām*: of creatures.

Translation

[If] in the sixth, [he is in] communion with Indra; in the seventh, he reaches the seat of Vishnu, and then, in the eighth, Rudra, lord of [all] creatures.

Commentary

If he passes in the sixth, he goes to the realm of *Indra*, which is *Swarga*, or heaven, where righteous souls dwell in paradise. If he passes in the seventh, he reaches the place of Viṣṇu, which is *Vaikuntha,* the supreme abode, where liberated souls dwell in oneness. If he passes in the eighth, he goes to the world of *Rudra*, the lord of all, which is also known as Śivaloka. This is the highest and most subtle world of existence, pervaded by the absolute reality, which is beyond mind, timeless and eternal.

Verse 16: During the ninth, tenth, eleventh or twelfth

नवम्यां तु महर्लोकं दशम्यां तु जनं व्रजेत् ।

एकादश्यां तपोलोकं द्वादश्यां ब्रह्म शाश्वतम् ।।१६।।

navamyāṃ tu maharlokaṃ daśamyāṃ tu janaṃ vrajet
ekādaśyāṃ tapolokaṃ dvādashyāṃ brahma śāśvatam (16)

Anvay

navamyām: in the ninth; *vrajet*: he reaches; *tu*: and; *daśamyām*: in the tenth; *ekādaśyām*: in the eleventh; *dvādashyām*: in the twelfth; *śāśvatam*: everlasting.

Translation

[If] in the ninth, he reaches, *mahaloka*; and in the tenth, *janoloka*; in the eleventh, *tapoloka*; in the twelfth, everlasting Brahma.

Commentary

If he passes in the ninth, he reaches *Mahaloka*, the sphere of great saints, sages and rishis. If he passes in the tenth, he goes to Janoloka, the plane of creativity, where pure-minded, liberated souls dwell. If he passes in the eleventh, he reaches Tapoloka, the place where yogis and ascetics, who have burned away all vestiges of attachment and illusion dwell. If he passes in the twelfth, he reaches brahma or satyaloka, the realm of absolute reality and truth.

Verse 17: Śiva and Aum

ततः परतरं शुद्धं व्यापकं निर्मलं शिवम् ।
सदोदितं परं ब्रह्म ज्योतिषामुदयो यतः ।।१७।।
tataḥ parataraṃ śuddhaṃ vyāpakaṃ nirmalaṃ śivam
sadoditaṃ paraṃ brahma jyotiṣāmudayo yataḥ (17)

Anvay

param brahma: Supreme Consciousness; *yataḥ*: which; *udayaḥ*: rises; *jyotiṣām*: from light; *sadā*: always; *uditam*: declared; *śivam*: Śiva; *parataram tataḥ*: beyond these; *śuddham*: pure; *vyāpakam*: all-pervading; *nirmalam*: resplendent.

Translation

The supreme consciousness, which rises from light, is always declared [to be] Śiva [who is] beyond these [*mātrās*], pure, all-pervading [and] resplendent.

Commentary

Śiva, the *ādi* or first yogi, is equated with supreme consciousness, because he dwelled in this state continuously while living and also after leaving the body. The supreme consciousness is beyond all perception of mind, beyond name, form and idea, beyond time and space, and any kind of limitation or association. The only quality that remains at this level of consciousness is light, because it arises from light. This is not the light of the sun, moon or stars, but a spiritual, pure and resplendent light. The supreme consciousness, also known as Śiva, that arises from this light, is said to be beyond the vibration of *Aum* and its syllables, whether taken individually or collectively. The *praṇāva* arises from Śiva, because pure consciousness is the source of all existence, and at the same time, beyond it.

Verse 18: Entry into Śiva consciousness

अतीन्द्रियं गुणातीतं मनो लीनं यदा भवेत् ।
अनूपमं शिवं शान्तं योगयुक्तं सदाविशेत् ॥१८॥
atīndriyaṃ guṇātītaṃ mano līnaṃ yadā bhavet
anūpamaṃ śivaṃ śāntaṃ yogayuktaṃ sadāviśet (18)

Anvay

yadā: when; *manaḥ*: mind; *bhavet*: is; *līnam*: absorbed; *ati-indriyam*: beyond the *indriyas*, senses; *guṇātītam*: beyond the *guṇas*, qualities; *sadā*: always; *yoga-yuktam*: immersed in *yoga*; *āviśet*: he should enter; *anūpamam*: incomparable; *śāntam*: auspicious; *śivam*: Śiva, cosmic consciousness.

Translation

When the mind is absorbed beyond the *indriyas* [and] the *guṇas*, [then], always immersed in yoga, he should enter the incomparable auspicious Śiva.

Commentary

It is interesting to note here that yoga refers to a high state of meditation, and not the practices of āsana and praṇāyāma, as we find today. In the science of yoga, there are several stages or states of meditation, which begin with withdrawal of the senses from the outside world. The word *indriya*, means 'sensory organs' and guṇa, is the 'nature' or 'quality' of the objects in the world. In ordinary life, a person is constantly attracted by the mind and senses to the objects, people and places of the world. In this way, it becomes difficult to internalise and discover the consciousness that is behind the mind.

Hence, in order to realise one's own true nature, it is

necessary to withdraw the senses from the external objects, and focus the mind and awareness within. This is the first and most important stage of meditation, or yoga. When this stage is mastered, through control of the senses, then the following stages of meditation will arise effortlessly. Thus follows the teaching on yoga. When the mind is absorbed beyond the sensory organs and their attraction to the nature of worldly objects, one remains immersed in yoga. Through this immersion, one should enter the subtle and incomparable state of pure consciousness, also known as the auspicious Śiva.

Verse 19: Important advice regarding meditation

तद्युक्तस्तन्मयो जन्तुः शनैर्मुञ्चेत्कलेवरम् ।
संस्थितो योगचारेण सर्वसङ्गविवर्जितः ।।१९।।
tadyuktastanmayo jantuḥ śanairmuñcetkalevaram
saṃsthito yogacāreṇa sarvasaṅgavivarjitaḥ (19)

Anvay

jantuḥ: person; *yuktaḥ*: established; *tanmayaḥ*: absorbed; *tat*: in it; *śanaiḥ*: slowly; *muñcet*: should relinquish; *kalevaram*: support; *saṃsthitaḥ*: intent upon; *yoga-cāreṇa*: observance of *yoga*; *vivarjitaḥ*: avoiding; *sarva saṅga*: all company.

Translation

The person [who is] established [there and] absorbed in it, should slowly relinquish support, intent upon the observance of yoga, avoiding all company.

Commentary

When one has gained mastery of the senses, and is able to turn them inward at will, it becomes possible to enter the field of mind and consciousness directly. It may be that in ancient times the mind was less active than it is today. However, for a person living in the modern world, it will take some time to free the mind from the disturbing influence of all the outer expectations and associations. This is followed by a stage, where one must make friends with the mind, and allow it to express itself in a non-judgemental way. The awareness must get to know the mind with all of its foibles, weaknesses and strengths. By accepting the mind and allowing it freedom to respond and react to the patterns stored within, in its own time and way, the mental field gradually becomes calm and still by itself. This is the missing key for meditators in this day and age, when the mind is field of mind and consciousness directly. It may be that in ancient times the mind was less active than it is today. However, for a person living in the modern world, it will take some time to free the mind from the disturbing influence of all the outer expectations and associations. This is followed by a stage, where one must make friends with the mind, and allow it to express itself in a non-judgemental way. The awareness must get to know the mind with all of its foibles, weaknesses and strengths. By accepting the mind and allowing it freedom to respond and react to the patterns stored within, in its own time and way, the mental field gradually becomes calm and still by itself. This is the missing key for meditators in this day and age, when the mind is over-externalised, overdeveloped and overactive from a very early age.

The mind that is allowed to find its own peace and harmony within, slowly subsides, and gives way to the subtle field of consciousness, which lies just beyond it. In this way, the person who becomes established and absorbed in this field is said to be master of the mind. This is the yogic way of meditation, which very few have understood. For such a person, the following advice is given. Having entered the space of consciousness, one should gradually leave aside the craving for entertainment and support of external people, places and things. Intent upon the observance of yoga, which here refers to the meditative experience, he should avoid all company and distractions, which will disturb the mind and divert it from this state higher consciousness.

Verse 20: Freedom from worldly duties

ततो विलीनपाशो ऽसौ विपलः कमलाप्रभुः ।
तेनैव ब्रह्मभावेन परमानन्दमश्नुते ।।२०।।

tato vilīnapāśo 'sau vipalaḥ kamalāprabhuḥ
tenaiva brahmabhāvena paramānandamaśnute (20)

Anvay

tataḥ: then; *vipalaḥ*: instant; *asau*: that person; *vilīna*: is freed from; *pāśaḥ*: bonds; *kamalā*: riches; *prabhuḥ*: marriage; *tena eva*: thus; *aśnute*: he attains; *param-ānandam*: Supreme Bliss; *brahma-bhāvena*: by absorption in Brahma.

Translation

Then, the instant that person is freed from the bonds [of] riches [and] marriage, he thus attains supreme bliss by absorption in Brahma.

Commentary

In early times it was incumbent on young persons to marry and propagate. Even the young sons of rishis and yogis were compelled to fulfil this duty. Family life is very demanding and causes constant upheaval, both externally and internally. Further, it was necessary for the son to assume responsibility for the family estate, properties, and wealth. This would have involved a major commitment to ensure that all the assets were managed properly, with no damages or losses incurred. So, there would be plenty of worry and anxiety. A person in this situation may practice meditation from time to time, but it would be difficult to establish oneself in the higher states of consciousness, and still fulfil these obligations. Hence, the moment one is freed from the bonds of wealth and marriage, one should live as a yogi, avoiding associations and distractions, and devote oneself to the attainment of supreme bliss, by absorption in the pure consciousness.

Verse 21: Acceptance of prārabdha

आत्मानं सततं ज्ञात्वा कालं नय महामते ।
प्रारब्धमखिलं भुञ्जन्नोद्वेगं कर्तुमर्हसि ॥२१॥

ātmānaṃ satataṃ jñātvā kālaṃ naya mahāmate
prārabdhamakhilaṃ bhuñjannodvegaṃ kartumarhasi (21)

Anvay

mahāmate: o Intelligent One; *naya*: spend; *kālam*: time; *satatam*: continually; *jñātvā*: knowing; *ātmānam*: Self; *bhuñjan*: enjoying; *akhilam*: entire; *prārabdham*: unavoidable results of past actions; *na*: without; *arhasi*: trying; *udvegam kartum*: to resist.

Translation

O Intelligent One, spend your time continually knowing the self, enjoying [your] entire *prārabdha*, without trying to resist [it].

Commentary

When ignorant persons retire from the work force, and are freed from worldly duties, they do not know how to utilise their time. They waste this valuable opportunity to be unencumbered by employment and family obligations. Meeting friends, watching TV, playing games, arguing with relations, drinking and attending social events, they attempt to while away the time. The intelligent person is one who realises the importance of this last stage of life, when it is possible to achieve the spiritual goals, which could not be attained earlier. Therefore, he is exhorted here to utilise his freedom properly. Spend this time alone, live simply in a peaceful environment, study spiritual texts, turn the awareness within, and know the self.

When the mind and senses are introverted, many memories and *saṃskāras*, impressions of the past, arise. One should allow these memories to surface and enjoy reliving one's entire past, without trying to judge or resist it. Similarly, the past is also responsible for many situations, actions and events, which must play out in one's current lifetime. These are the *prārabdha*, destined karmas, which are unavoidable, and must be fulfilled in order to move on. So, one should accept these karmas, when they arise, and experience them without any regrets. In this way the negativity and attachments that obstruct the higher vision are removed, and one can easily sail into the elevated sphere of consciousness.

Verses 22 and 23a: Tattvajñāna and prārabdha

उत्पन्ने तत्त्वविज्ञाने प्रारब्धं नैव मुञ्चति ।

तत्त्वज्ञानोदयादूर्ध्वं प्रारब्धं नैव विद्यते ।।२२।।

देहादीनामसत्त्वात्तु यथा स्वप्ने विबोधतः ।२३।

utpanne tattvavijñāne prārabdhaṃ naiva muñcati
tattvajñānodayādūrdhvaṃ prārabdhaṃ naiva vidyate (22)
dehādīnāmasattvāttu yathā svapne vibodhataḥ (23a)

Anvay

eva: even; *tattva-vijñāne*: when knowledge of the *tattvas*, true essence; *utpanne*: has emerged; *prārabdhaṃ*: unavoidable results of past actions; *na muñcati*: does not leave; *tu*: but; *na eva vidyate*: he is not affected by; *prārabdhaṃ*: unavoidable results of past actions; *udayāt-ūrdhvaṃ*: rising up; *tattvajñāna*: *tattvajñāna*, knowledge of the elements or underlying truth; *asattvāt*: because of the unreal nature; *deha-ādīnām*: of the body and other [material things]; *yathā*: as if; *vibodhataḥ*: perceived; *svapne*: in a dream.

Translation

Even when knowledge of the *tattvas* has emerged, prārabdha does not leave [him], but he is not affected by prārabdha [after] the rising up [of] *tattvajñāna*, because of the unreal nature of the body and other [material things], as if perceived in a dream.

Commentary

The term *tattwajñāna* was used frequently in early times to denote the quality of a seer, or visionary: one who was capable of seeing into the essence of existence. The word *tattwa* refers to the five basic elements: earth, water, fire, air and ether, which comprise all beings in the material world. In this sense, the five elements are not things in themselves, but elemental energies. For example, the energy of earth is solid and heavy. The energy of water is fluid. The energy of fire is hot and volatile. The energy of air is gaseous and kinetic. The energy of ether is vacuous and still.

Normally, a person sees only the appearance of things, and understands them accordingly. But a tattwajñāni is able to see behind the appearances, and to know how these energies are actively combining and transforming everywhere and in everything from moment to moment. Even the yogi, who has attained this knowledge of the tattwa, must undergo the prārabdha, destined karmas, in order to eliminate them. However, they do not affect him after the state of tattvajñāna arises. He experiences the unreal nature and appearance of the body, objects and events in life, as ephemeral and unreal, like in a dream.

Verses 23b and 24a: Prārabdha and rebirth

कर्म जन्मान्तरीयं यत्प्रारब्धमिति कीर्तितम् ।।२३।।
तत्तु जन्मान्तराभावात्पुंसो नैवास्ति कर्हिचित ।२४।
karma janmāntarīyaṃ yatprārabdhamiti kīrtitam (23b)
tattu janmāntarābhāvātpuṃso naivāsti karhicit (24a)

Anvay

yat karma: that *karma*, results of actions; *janmāntarīyaṃ*: associated with former births; *iti kīrtitam*: is called; *prārabdham*: unavoidable results of past actions; *tu*: yet; *puṃsaḥ*: person; *janmāntarābhāvāt*: who has no rebirth; *na . . karhicit*: never; *asti*: experiences; *yat*: it.

Translation

That *karma* associated with former births is called *prārabdha.* Yet the person who has no rebirth never experiences it.

Commentary

Prārabdha are the destined karmas that were performed in the past during former births, but have come to fruition in the present birth. However, that person, who is free from rebirth, will never undergo them. This is freedom from the bondage of karma, which only the liberated soul can attain.

Verses 24b and 25a: What is the source of illusion?

स्वप्नदेहो यथाध्यस्तस्तथैवायं हि देहकः ।।२४।।

अध्यस्तस्य कुतो जन्म जन्माभावे कुतः स्थितिः ।२५।

svapnadeho yathādhyastastathaivāyaṃ hi dehakaḥ (24b)
ādhyastasya kuto janma janmābhāve kutaḥ sthitiḥ (25a)

Anvay

yathā: as; *svapna-dehaḥ*: body in a dream; *adhyaḥ*: illusory; *tathā*: so; *hi*: indeed; *ayam dehakaḥ*: this body; *kutaḥ*: where; *janma*: birth; *tasya*: of that; *adhyaḥ*: illusory; *kutaḥ*: where; *sthitiḥ*: does it exist; *janma-abhāve*: in the absence of rebirth.

Translation

As the body in a dream [is] illusory, so indeed [is] this body. Where [is] the birth of that [which is] illusory? Where does it exist in the absence of rebirth?

Commentary

At night, during dream, the body and the events that one experiences seem to be real. But, upon awakening and opening the eyes, one realises they were illusory. In the same way, for one who sees behind the appearances, this physical body is also illusory. What is the source of this illusion? From where does the unreal arise? Where does the body exist before rebirth, and where does it go after death?

Verses 25b and 26a: Where is the universe?

उपादानं प्रपञ्चस्य मृद्भाण्डस्येव पश्यति ।।२५।।

अज्ञानं चेति वेदान्तैस्तस्मिन्नष्टे क्व विश्वता ।२६।

upādānaṃ prapañcasya mṛdbhāṇḍasyeva paśyati (25b)
ajñānaṃ ceti vedāntaistasminnaṣṭe kva viśvatā (26a)

Anvay

paśyati: he sees; *vedāntaiḥ*: in accordance with Vedānta, non-dualism; *ajñāna*: spiritual ignorance; *upādānam*: material cause; *prapañcasya*: of the form; *mṛdbhāṇḍasya*: of the clay-pot; *ca*: and; *iti*: asks; *naṣte*: if . . is no more; *kva*: where; *tasmin*: then; *viśvatā*: universe.

Translation

He sees, in accordance with Vedānta, [that] *ajñāna* [is] the material cause of the form of the clay-pot, and asks, if *ajñāna* is no more, where then [is] the universe?

Commentary

Vedānta gives the analogy of *ajñāna*, ignorance in relation to the reality of consciousness, as the material cause of form; in the same way that clay is the material cause of the claypot. If ajñāna is no more than illusion, then where is the universe?

Verses 26b and 27: The snake and the rope

यथा रज्जुं परित्यज्य सर्पं गृह्णाति वै भ्रमात् ।।२६।।
तद्वत्सत्यमविज्ञाय जगत्पश्यति मूढधीः ।
रज्जुखण्डे परिज्ञाते सर्परूपं न तिष्ठति ।।२७।।

yathā rajjuṃ parityajya sarpaṃ gṛhṇati vai bhramāt (26)
tadvatsatyamavijñāya jagatpaśyati mūdhadhīḥ
rajjukhaṇḍe parijñāte sarparūpaṃ na tiṣṭhati. (27)

Anvay

yathā: just as; *gṛhṇati*: he considers; *parityajya*: from a distance; *rajjum*: rope; *sarpam*: snake; *tadvat*: in the same way; *avijñāya*: not knowing; *satyam*: truth; *mūdhadhīḥ*: fool; *paśyati*: sees; *jagat*: world; *brahmāt*: separate from Brahma; *parijñāte*: when he recognises; *rajju-khaṇḍe*: piece of rope; *sarpa-rūpam*: appearance [of] a snake; *na tiṣṭhati*: does not remain.

Translation

Just as he considers from a distance a rope [to be] a snake, in the same way, not knowing the truth, the fool sees the world [as] separate from Brahma. When he recognises [it] as a piece [of] rope, the appearance [of] a snake does not remain.

Commentary

While walking at night, gazing ahead into the distance, one becomes frightened to glimpse a snake, moving slowly across the road. However, as one continues to walk, the snake turns out to be a rope that was dropped by someone. In the same way, the ignorant person, whose perception is clouded by *ajñāna*, sees the material world as a separate reality from consciousness. But when the light of consciousness dawns, one sees the world as part of consciousness, and consciousness as part of the world. Just as, when the length of rope is seen clearly, the illusion of a snake no longer remains; so the illusion of duality, the material world as separate from consciousness, is gone.

Verses 28 and 29a: Purpose of prārabdha

अधिष्ठाने तथा ज्ञाते प्रपञ्चे शून्यतां गते ।
देहस्यापि प्रपञ्चत्वात्प्रारब्धावस्थितिः कुतः ।।२८।।
अज्ञानजनबोधार्थं प्रारब्धमिति चोच्यते ।२९।

adhiṣṭhāne tathā jñāte prapañce śūnyatāṃ gate
dehasyāpi prapañcatvātprārabdhāvasthitiḥ kutaḥ (28)
ajñānajanabodhārthaṃ prārabdhamiti cocyate (29a)

Anvay

tathā: thus; *jñāte*: when he knows; *śūnyatām*: emptiness; *prapañce gate*: when the material support has gone; *kutaḥ*: where; *avasthitiḥ*: abode; *prārabdha*: *prārabdha*, unavoidable results of past actions; *dehasya*: body; *api*: also; *prapañcatvāt*: as . . is of the phenomenal world; *ca*: and; *iti ucyate*: so it is said; *bodha-artham*: for the purpose of teachings; *jana*: those born in; *ajñāna*: spiritual ignorance.

Translation

Thus, when he knows emptiness, when the material support has gone, where [is] the abode [of] prārabdha, as the body is also of the phenomenal world. And so it is said prārabdha [is] for the purpose of teaching those born in *ajñāna.*

Commentary

The field of consciousness exists everywhere, behind everything, in the dimension of space. The quality of space is all pervading emptiness or void. When the yogi is able to transcend the mind and body, and merge his awareness in consciousness, he experiences this emptiness directly. The material support for the consciousness is the mind and body, and the outside world experienced through the senses. When the awareness is merged in consciousness, however, this support is gone and there is nothing…no objective reality upon which to base the mind. Hence the question arises, where is the source or the abode of prārabdha, the destined karmas, as the body is part of the phenomenal world, and the prārabdha are expressed and fulfilled through the physical existence.

The prārabdha exist along with the other karmas in the karmic storehouse, which is a part of *citta*, the individual field of consciousness. Although the prārabdha must be expressed, the yogi who is established in consciousness, is freed from their influence or control. He thus creates and determines his own destiny from moment to moment, unhampered by limitations and conditioning from the past. And so, it is said that the prārabdha karmas exist for the purpose of teaching those, who are born in *ajñāna*, ignorance of the higher reality of consciousness, by generating the experiences of duality, such as pain and pleasure, success and failure, wealth and poverty, and so on, until these lessons are learned.

Verses 29b and 30: Self realisation

ततः कालवशादेव प्रारब्धे तु क्षयं गते ।।२९।।

ब्रह्मप्रणवसंधानो नादो ज्योतिर्मयः शिवः ।

स्वयमाविर्भवेदात्मा मेघापाये ऽशुमानिव ।।३०।।

tataḥ kālavaśādeva prārabdhe tu kṣayaṃ gate (29b)
brahmapraṇavasaṃdhāno nādo jyotirmayaḥ śivaḥ
svayamāvirbhavedātmā meghāpāye 'śumāniva (30)

Anvay

tataḥ: then; *prārabdhe kṣayam gate*: when *prārabdha* has come to an end; *kālavaśāt*: in the course of time; *ātmā*: *ātman*, Self beyond mind and body; *śivaḥ*: auspicious; *nādaḥ*: sound; *jyotirmayaḥ*: consisting of light; *saṃdhānaḥ*: uniting; *praṇava*: *praṇava*, primal sound vibration; *brahma*: *brahma*, source of existence; *āśumān*: quickly; *svayam-aviḥ-bhavet*: reveals itself; *iva*: like; *megha-apāye*: when the clouds disperse.

Translation

Then, in the course of time, when *prārabdha* have come to an end, the *ātman*, [which is] the auspicious sound consisting of light [and] uniting *praṇava* [with] *brahma*, quickly reveals itself, like [the sun] when the clouds disperse.

Commentary

The yogi who is established in consciousness gradually frees himself from the cycle of karma by disengaging with unnecessary worldly involvement and cultivating non-attachment in all interactions. The prārabdha, destined karmas, will only come to an end if there is cessation of further karmas. This is the real reason for renunciation. In the absence of renunciation, the karmas will simply go on building, and the mature karmas will go on expressing, as prārabdha. In this sense, yoga is much more than a practice. It is a way of life, of living consciously, which ultimately leads to liberation from the bondage of karma.

So that, in the course of time, when the prārabdha have come to an end, the ātman, or pure self, is revealed. Here, the ātman is described as the auspicious sound vibration, *siva nāda*, consisting of light and light everywhere. It is that subtle point of transformation, where pure vibration enters the space of consciousness and fills it with luminosity. In this way, the ātman unites *Praṇava*, the Omkāra, with *Brahma*, the source of existence, and quickly reveals itself, like the blazing sun, when the clouds are dispersed.

Verse 31: Nāda yoga

सिद्धासने स्थितो योगी मुद्रां संधाय वैष्णवीं ।
शृणुयाद्दक्षिणे कर्णे नादमन्तर्गतं सदा ॥३१॥

siddhāsane sthito yogī mudrāṃ saṃdhāya vaiṣṇavīm
śṛṇuyāddakṣiṇe karṇe nādamantargataṃ sadā (31)

Anvay

yogī: *yogin*, yoga adept; *sthitaḥ*: seated; *siddhāsane*: in *siddhāsana*, accomplished pose; *saṃdhāya*: having adopted; *vaiṣṇavīm mudrām*: posture of Viṣṇu; *śṛṇuyāt*: hears; *nādam*: *nāda*, subtle sound vibration; *sadā*: always; *antar-gatam*: goes into; *dakṣiṇe karṇe*: right ear.

Translation

The yogin, seated in *siddhāsana*, having adopted the *vishnu mudrā*, hears the *nāda* [which] always goes into the right ear.

Commentary

Siddhāsana is the classical locked meditation asana in which the position of the heels places pressure on both the mūladhāra and swadhisthana cakras. This continuous pressure allows the reproductive energies from these centres to be redirected upward through the suṣumnā pathway to the brain for the purpose of higher meditation.

Viṣṇu mudrā, also known as *nasagra mudrā*, is the hand position commonly employed for controlling the nasal flows, during the practice of prāṇāyāma. In this practice, the index and middle fingers of the right hand are folded forward, so that the tips touch the palm at the base of the thumb. The thumb, ring finger and little finger remain stretched. The hand is then raised in front of the face, so that the nasal passages can be controlled by pressing the right nostril with the thumb, and the left nostril with the ring and little fingers.

The yogi should master the practice of prāṇāyāma, before engaging in nāda yoga, so that breath retention can be performed without any difficulty or strain.

Technique

Chose a quiet and clean environment to begin the practice of nada yoga. Sit in siddhāsana, or any comfortable meditation posture, and allow the body to become calm and still. Practise slow rhythmic breathing, gradually elongating the breath. Place the right hand in viṣṇu mudrā and raise it in front of the face.

Inhale slowly and deeply through both nostrils. Close both nostrils by pressing them gently with the thumb and ring fingers. Holding the breath inside for a comfortable period, focus on sound at the right ear. Whatever sound comes to your attention, focus on that sound, whether it is an outer sound or an inner sound. As you focus on the first sound, allow it to draw your attention to the next sound.

As soon as you begin to feel breathless, release the pressure on the nostrils and slowly exhale. Inhale again slowly through both nostrils, retain the breath, and focus the awareness on sound at the right ear. With practice, you will find that the sounds gradually become finer, so that each sound draws the awareness inward to a subtler and subtler sound.

Verse 32: Inner sound

अभ्यस्यमानो नादो ऽयं बाह्यमावृणुते ध्वनिः ।
पक्षाद्विपक्षमखिलं जित्वा तुर्यपदंव्रजेत् ।।३२।।

abhyasyamāno nādo 'yam bāhyamāvṛṇute dhvaniḥ
pakṣādvipakṣamakhilaṃ jitvā turyapadaṃ vrajet. (32)

Anvay

ayam: this; *dhvaniḥ*: sound; *nādaḥ*: inner tone; *mānaḥ*: aim; *abhyasya*: of the practice; *āvṛṇute*: is hidden from; *bāhyam*: outer; *jitvā*: having conquered; *akhilam vipakṣam*: all obstacles; *vrajet*: he enters; *turya-padam*: fourth state, superconsciousness; *pakṣāt*: in fifteen days.

Translation

This sound, [whose] inner tone [is] the aim of the practice, is hidden from the outer. Having conquered all obstacles, he enters the fourth state in fifteen days.

Commentary

The aim of nāda yoga is to allow the vibration of sound to draw the awareness inward to subtler and subtler sounds. Normally, these inner sounds are not perceptible by the senses or even by the mind. So, the verse says that they are hidden from the outer senses. However, we are all born with inner senses, which connect the mind with the outer senses. The inner senses function at a psychic or subconscious level, and it is through these senses that we perceive the inner worlds of dream, vision and imagination. In fact, these inner senses are quite active in small children, although as adults, we are unable to perceive them directly, and so do not develop them.

An important aim of yoga and meditation is to develop and awaken these inner senses, because they are the stuff of real creativity and genius. So, it is in nāda yoga, we aim to develop the inner sense of hearing in order to perceive the subtle sound vibrations, which exist unheard within us and all around us, at all times. By developing the inner sense of hearing, the awareness is easily led into the subtler states of consciousness, where these sounds are hidden. In this way, the normal obstacles of the mind, such as thoughts, memories, restlessness, tiredness, are overcome, and the meditator easily enters the transcendental state of samadhi, which is the fourth state of consciousness, within fifteen days.

Verses 33 to 35: Sounds heard in nāda yoga

श्रूयते प्रथमाभ्यासे नादो नानाविधो महान् ।

वर्धमाने तथाभ्यासे श्रूयते सूक्षमसूक्षमतः ।।३३।।

आदौ जलधिजीमूतभेरीनिर्झरसंभवः ।

मध्ये मर्दलशब्दाभो घण्टाकाहलजस्तथा ।।३४।।

अन्ते तु किकिणीवंशवीणाभ्रमरनिस्वनः ।

इति नानाविधा नादाः श्रूयन्ते सूक्ष्मसूक्ष्मतः ।।३५।।

śrūyate prathamābhyāse nādo nānāvidho mahān
vardhamāne tathābhyāse śrūyate sūkṣmasūkṣmataḥ (33)
ādau jaladhijīmūtabherīnirjharasaṃbhavaḥ
madhye mardalaśabdābho ghaṇṭākāhalajastathā (34)
ante tu kikiṇīvaṃśavīṇābhramaranisvanaḥ
iti nānāvidhā nādāḥ śrūyante sūkṣmasūkṣmataḥ (35)

Anvay

prathama-abhyāse: at the beginning of his practice; *śrūyate*: he hears; *nānāvidhaḥ*: many; *mahān*: loud; *nādaḥ*: sounds; *tathā*: then; *abhyāse vardhamāne*: as his practice increases; *śrūyate*: he hears; *sūkṣma*: more subtle; *sūkṣmataḥ*: scarcely audible; *ādau*: at first; *saṃbhavaḥ*: source; *jaladhi*: ocean; *jīmūta*: clouds; *bherī*: kettle-drums; *nirjhara*: waterfalls; *tathā*: then; *madhye*: in the middle; *ābhaḥ*: like; *śabda*: sounds; *jaḥ*: caused by; *mardala*: drums; *ghantā*: bells; *kāhala*: horns; *ante*: at the last stage; *nisvanaḥ*: sounds; *kikiṇīḥ*: small bells; *vaṃśaḥ*: flutes; *vīṇāḥ*: Indian lutes; *bhramara*: *nānāvidhāḥ nādāḥ*: various sounds; *śrūyante*: are heard; *sūkṣmasūkṣmataḥ*: more and more subtle.

Translation

At the beginning of his practice he hears many loud sounds;

then, as his practice increases, he hears [them as] more subtle, [until] scarcely audible. At first the source [of the sounds seems to be from] the ocean, clouds, kettle-drums [and] waterfalls; then, in the middle [stage], [they are] like sounds caused by drums, bells [and] horns. At the last stage [there are] sounds [of] small bells, flutes, lutes [and] bees. Thus various sounds are heard, [becoming] more and more subtle.

Commentary

Nāda yoga is an ancient form of meditation, which was developed by yogis, who lived and practised in natural environments, such as forests, mountains, river banks and nearby lakes and oceans. Hence, many of the sounds that they heard and related to in meditation were the external sounds of nature. At the beginning of the practice, loud sounds could be heard from outside, such as the blowing of the wind, the crack of thunder, the flow of rivers and waterfalls, the lap of waves on the shore, the singing of birds. But as the practice developed, the sounds became more subtle, until they were scarcely audible.

Then in the middle stage, they heard such sounds as the beating of drums, the ringing of bells, and the blowing of horns. Then in the last state, the sounds became very subtle, such as the tinkling of tiny bells, melodic notes played on flute, plucking of the lute, and buzzing of bees. These various sounds were heard at different times during the practice, and became more and more subtle, as the meditator delved deeply within. The important aspect of utilising sound as a method of meditation was that it gave a firm basis for the mind, which the awareness could follow inward, and which kept the attention from wandering away from the practice of meditation into unknown areas of the deep consciousness.

Verse 36: Sound of the drum

महति श्रूयमाणे तु महाभेर्यादिकध्वनौ ।
तत्र सूक्ष्मं सूक्ष्मतरं नादमेव परामृशेत् ।।३६।।

mahati śrūyamāne tu mahābheryādikadhvanau
tatra sūkṣmam sūkṣmatram nādameva parāmṛśet (36)

Anvay

ādika: at first; *mahati dhvanau*: when the lound sound; *mahābherī*: great drum; *śrūyamāne*: is heard; *tatra*: then; *eva parāmṛśet*: he should just concentrate on; *sūkṣmam sūkṣmataram*: most subtle; *nādam*: sounds.

Translation

When at first the loud sound [of] the great drum is heard, then he should just concentrate on its most subtle sounds.

Commentary

There are certain sounds that were heard frequently during the practice of nāda yoga. One of these is the sound of the drum. In ancient times the villagers and forest dwellers communicated with one another over long distances by playing certain rhythms on large drums. They also played drums during their rituals and get togethers. Sometimes the drumming would go on for many hours. When the loud sound of the great drum was heard during meditation, it would be very overpowering and disturb the practice. Hence, the advice is given here to ignore the loud beating sound, and focus on its most subtle derivative sounds.

Verses 37 and 38: Focusing on one sound

घनमुत्सृज्य वा सूक्ष्मे सूक्ष्ममुत्सृज्य वा घने ।
रममाणमपि क्षिप्तं मनो नान्यत्र चालयेत् ॥३७॥
यत्र कुत्रापि वा नादे लगति प्रथमं मनः ।
तत्र तत्र स्थिरीभूत्वा तेन सार्धं विलीयते ॥३८॥

ghanamutsṛjya vā sūkṣme sūkṣmamutsṛjya vā ghane
ramamāṇamapi kṣiptaṃ mano nānyatra cālayet (37)
yatra kutrāpi vā nāde lagati prathamaṃ manaḥ
tatra tatra sthirībhūtvā tena sārdhaṃ vilīyate (38)

Anvay

vā . . vā: either . . or; *utsṛjya*: leaving; *ghanam*: gross sound; *sūkṣme*: for the subtle; *sūkṣmam*: subtle sound; *ghane*: for the gross; *api*: even; *ramamānam*: while delighting; *manaḥ*: mind; *kṣiptam*: distracted; *na cālayet*: should not be moved; *anyatra*: to other [sounds]; *vā api*: or even; *yatra kutra*: whichever; *nāde*: sound; *manaḥ*: mind; *prathamam*: first; *lagati*: attaches itself to; *sārdham*: securely; *sthirībhūtvā*: fixed; *tatra tatra*: there; *vilīyate*: it becomes absorbed; *tena*: in it.

Translation

Either leaving the gross sound for the subtle, or leaving the subtle sound for the gross, even while delighting [in them], the mind [becomes] distracted, [and so] should not be moved to other [sounds]. Or whichever sound the mind first attaches itself to, securely fixed there, it becomes absorbed in it.

Commentary

Nāda yoga is primarily a practice of dhāraṇa, one pointed concentration. When the perception of inner sound has been established, it is then necessary to focus on one sound to the exclusion of all the others, just as one would focus on one symbol or one mantra. Otherwise, if the attention leaves the one sound, whether for a more gross or subtle sound, or a pleasing sound, it becomes distracted. The best way to progress in the practice is to fix the mind on whatever sound it first becomes attached to, so that it becomes absorbed in it, and does not even hear any other sound.

Verse 39: Absorption into space

विस्मृत्य सकलं बाह्यं नादे दुग्धाम्बुवन्मनः ।
एकीभूयाथ सहसा चिदाकाशे विलीयते ।।३९।।

vismṛtya sakalaṃ bāhyaṃ nāde dugdhāmbuvanmanaḥ
ekībhūyātha sahasā cidākāśe vilīyate (39)

Anvay

vismṛtya: having forgotten; *sakalam*: all; *bāhyam*: external; *manaḥ*: mind; *ekībhūyātha*: uniting; *nāde*: with the sound; *dugdha*: milk; *āmbuvan*: water; *sahasā*: immediately; *vilīyate*: is absorbed; *cidākāśe*: in *cidākāśa*, inner space of consciousness.

Translation

Having forgotten all external [experiences], the mind, uniting with the sound [as] milk [with] water, is immediately absorbed in *cidākāśa*.

Commentary

This absorption of the awareness into sound, leads to the experience of *cidākāśa*, absorption of the mind into the dimension of space. In this state, the mind is merged with the sound, just as milk is merged with water, and all experiences of the external world are forgotten. There is just the spacial dimension, filled with the vibration of sound, and nothing else.

Verse 40: Sound meditation

उदासीनस्ततो भूत्वा सदाभ्यासेन सम्यमी ।
उन्मनीकारकं सद्यो नादमेवावधारयेत् ।।४०।।

udāsīnastato bhūtvā sadābhyāsena samyamī
unmanīkārakam sadyo nādamevāvadhārayet (40)

Anvay

tataḥ: then; *bhūtvā*: having become; *udāsīnaḥ*: indifferent to; *unmanīkārakam*: passion; *sadā ābhyāsena*: by the continual practice; *samyamī*: self-control; *sadyaḥ*: at once; *eva avadhārayet*: he should give his full attention to; *nādam*: inner sound.

Translation

Then, having become indifferent to passion by the continual practice [of] self-control, he should at once give his full attention to the inner sound.

Commentary

The normal state of consciousness, whether waking or dreaming, is continually distracted by desires, whether unfulfilled or in the process of being fulfilled. For this reason, it is virtually impossible for the untrained mind to hold the attention steady on one object or sound. In order to succeed in meditation, it is necessary to undergo a period of preparation, whereby the lifestyle, ethics and mental patterns are cultivated, which will allow the practitioner to free the mind from its attraction to desire and attachment. Once indifference to desire has been achieved through the continual practice of self-control, one should immediately give his full attention to the meditation on inner sound.

Verse 41: Absorption in sound

सर्वचिन्तां समुत्सृज्य सर्व चेष्टाविवर्जितः ।
नादमेवानुसंदध्यान्नादे चित्तं विलीयते ।।४१।।

sarvacintāṃ samutsṛjya sarva ceṣṭāvivarjitaḥ
nādamevānusaṃdadhyānnāde cittaṃ vilīyate (41)

Anvay

samutsṛjya: having abandoned; *sarva-cintām*: every thought; *ca*: and; *avivarjitaḥ*: renounced; *sarva iṣṭa*: every desire; *eva anusaṃdadhyāt*: he should place all his attention on; *nādam*: inner sound; *cittaṃ vilīyate*: until his consciousness becomes absorbed; *nāde*: in the sound.

Translation

Having abandoned every thought and renounced every desire, he should place all his attention on the inner sound, until his consciousness becomes absorbed in it.

Commentary

When the mind is left to its own devices, thoughts and desires arise continually and distract the awareness. Nāda yoga is a practice of concentration, which requires the awareness to remain focused and free from every thought and desire. In order to achieve this state, practice is required. One must be able to observe and understand the patterns and the habits of the mind, before it can be brought into a steady, one-pointed focus. In order to achieve this state, it is helpful to follow the various sounds, as they manifest, outside and inside, from gross to subtle. However, once the mind is free from thought and desire, the practitioner should focus his entire attention on the one inner sound, until his consciousness becomes totally absorbed in it.

Verses 42 and 43a: Quality of absorption

मकरन्दं पिबन्भृङ्गो गन्धान्नापेक्षते यथा ।
नादासक्तं सदा चित्तं विषयं न हि काङ्क्षति ।।४२।।
बद्धः सुनादगन्धेन सद्यः संत्यक्तचापलः ।४३।
makarandaṃ pibanbhṛṅgo gandhānnāpekṣate yathā
nādāsaktaṃ sadā cittaṃ viṣayaṃ na hi kāṅkṣati (42)
baddhaḥ sunādagandhena sadyaḥ saṃtyaktacāpalaḥ (43a)

Anvay

yathā: just as; *bhṛṅgaḥ*: bee; *piban*: drinking; *makarandam*: nectar; *na pekṣate*: is not concerned; *gandhāt*: with its fragrance; *hi*: so; *cittam*: consciousness; *sadā*: always; *nāda āsaktam*: intent on the *nāda*; *na kāṅkṣati*: does not crave; *viṣayam*: sensual enjoyment; *baddhaḥ*: bound; *su-nāda-gandhena*: by the *nāda*'s own sweet fragrance; *cāpalaḥ*: its fickle nature; *saṃtyakta*: relinquished.

Translation

Just as the bee drinking the nectar is not concerned with its fragrance, so the consciousness, always intent on the nāda, does not crave sensual enjoyment [as it is] bound by the nāda's own sweet fragrance, its fickle nature relinquished.

Commentary

Sound has a very powerful effect on the consciousness. We can see the immediate effect that music has on the emotions and the mood. In the same way, inner sound unifies and harmonises the vibrational field and holds the consciousness steady and still. When the consciousness is fixed on nāda, it remains focused and at ease in itself.

Verses 43b and 44a: One-pointed concentration on nāda

नादग्रहणतश्चित्तमन्तरङ्गभुजङ्गमः ।।४३।।

विस्मृत्य विश्वमेकाग्रः कुत्रचिन्न हि धावति ।४४।

nādagrahaṇataścittamantaraṅgabhujaṅgamaḥ (43b)
vismṛtya viśvamekāgraḥ kutracinna hi dhāvati (44a)

Anvay

antaraṅga bhujangamaḥ: inner serpent; *cittam*: consciousness; *nāda grahanataḥ*: holds the *nāda*; *ekāgraḥ*: concentrating; *vismṛtya*: unaware of; *viśvam*: all; *na hi dhāvati*: does not rush; *kutracit*: here and there.

Translation

The inner serpent [of] consciousness [which] holds the *nāda*, concentrating [on it], unaware of all [else], does not rush here and there.

Commentary

The inner serpent of consciousness, is the awareness, which tends to pull the mind and senses here and there, when it is undisciplined and has no steady point of focus. When the awareness is held by the nāda, it remains concentrated with little effort, and ceases to rush from one attraction to another.

Verses 44b to 46a: Nāda restrains the mind

मनोमत्तगजेन्द्रस्य विषयोद्यानचारिनः ।।४४।।
नियामनसमर्थो ऽयं निनादो मिशिताङ्कुशः ।
नादो ऽन्तरङ्गसारङ्गबन्धने वागुरायते ।।४५।।
अन्तरङ्गसमुद्रस्य रोधे वेलायते ऽपि वा ।४६।

nanomattagajendrasya viṣayodyānacārinaḥ (44b)
niyāmanasamartho 'yaṃ ninādo niśitāṅkuśaḥ
nādo 'ntaraṅgasāraṇgabandhane vāgurāyate (45)
antaraṅgasamudrasya rodhe velāyate 'pi vā (46a)

Anvay

ayam ninādaḥ: this sound; *niśita aṅkuśaḥ*: sharp hook; *samarthaḥ*: suitable for; *niyāmana*: restraining; *manaḥ*: mind; *matta-gajendrasya*: like a mad elephant; *cārinaḥ*: roaming; *udyāna*: pleasure garden; *viṣaya*: sensual enjoyment; *vāgurāyate*: ensnares; *bandhane*: as a fetter; *antaraṅga sāraṇga*: inner deer; *vā api*: or also; *velāyate*: is a shore; *rodhe*: which holds back; *antaraṅga-samudrasya*: inner ocean.

Translation

This sound [is] a sharp hook, suitable for restraining the mind [which is] like a mad elephant roaming the pleasure garden [of] sensual enjoyment. The nāda ensnares as a fetter [for] the inner deer, or is also a shore, which holds back the inner ocean.

Commentary

The nāda acts as a sharp hook to restrain the mind. Here the mind is described as a mad elephant, roaming the pleasure garden of the world, seeking one sensory enjoyment after another. The nāda holds the mind in the same way that a rope holds the deer, or the shore line holds back the ocean.

Verses 46b to 47a: Praṇava nāda

ब्रह्मप्रणवसंलग्ननादो ज्योतिर्मयात्मकः ।।४६।।

मनस्तत्र लयं याति तद्विष्णोः परं पदम् ।४७।

brahmapraṇavasaṃlagnanādo jyotirmayātmakaḥ (46b)
manastatra layaṃ yāti tadviṣṇoḥ paraṃ padam (47a)

Anvay

nādaḥ saṃlagna: *nāda* arising from; *praṇava*: *Praṇava*, Aum, primal sound vibration; *brahma*: *Brahma*, creative principle; *ātmakaḥ*: has the nature of; *jyotirmaya*: light; *tatra*: there; *manaḥ*: mind; *yāti layam*: becomes absorbed; *tat*: this; *param padam*: supreme seat; *viṣṇoḥ*: of Viṣṇu.

Translation

The nāda, arising from *Praṇava* [and] *Brahma*, has the nature of light. There the mind becomes absorbed. This [is] the supreme seat of Viṣṇu.

Commentary

Aum is the nāda arising from Praṇava and the pure consciousness of Brahma. Aum is the first vibration and has the quality of luminosity; therefore, the mind easily becomes absorbed in it. Aum is also the supreme seat of Viṣṇu, the divine consciousness, that sustains the creation.

Verses 47b to 48a: Space and sound

तावदाकाशसंकल्पो यावच्छब्दः प्रवर्तते ।।४७।।

निःशब्दं तत्परं ब्रह्म परमात्मा समीयते ।४८।

tāvadākāśasaṃkalpo yāvacchabdaḥ pravartate (47b)
niḥśabdaṃ tatparaṃ brahma paramātmā samīyate (48a)

Anvay

yāvat: as long as; *śabdaḥ*: sound; *pravartate*: is produced; *tāvat*: then; *ākāśa-saṃkalpaḥ*: will of *ākāśa*, ether element whose property is sound; *tat*: then; *paramātmā*: supreme self; *amīyate*: is equal to; *niḥśabdam*: soundless; *param brahma*: supreme Brahma, creator.

Translation

As long as sound is produced, then [there is] the will of *ākāśa*. Then the supreme self is equal to the soundless supreme Brahma.

Commentary

The basis of sound is vibration, and vibration is the basis of creation. *Ākāśa*, the infinite space, is the first element of creation. Being the first element of material existence, which will hold all the creation to come, ākāśa relates with *sankalpa*, the will to become. Ākāśa arises from the subtle essence of sound. In the manifest creation, sound travels through space. In the unmanifest dimension, *paramātmā*, the supreme self, is equal to *parambrahma*, the universal pure consciousness, which is the source of creation beyond sound.

Verses 48b to 51a: Beyond the mind

नादो यावन्मनस्तावन्नादान्ते ऽपि मनोन्मनी ।।४८।।
सशब्दश्चाक्षरे क्षीणे निःशब्दं परमं पदं
सदा नादानुसंधानात्संक्षीणा वासना तु या ।।४९।।
निरञ्जने विलीयेते मनोवायू न संशयः
नादकोटिसहस्राणि बिन्दुकोटिशतानि च ।।५०।।
सर्वे तत्र लयं यान्ति ब्रह्मप्रवनादके ।५१।

nādo yāvanmastāvannādānte 'pi manonmanī (48b)
saśabdaścākṣare kṣīṇe niḥśabdam paramaṃ padam
sadā nādānusaṃdhānātsaṃkṣīṇā vāsanā tu yā (49)
nirañjane vilīyete manovāyū na saṃśayaḥ
nādakoṭisahasrāṇi bindukoṭiśatāni ca (50)
sarve tatra layaṃ yānti brahmapravanādake (51a)

Anvay

yāvat: as long as; *manaḥ*: mind; *tāvat*: then; *nāda-ante*: at the end of *nāda*; *manonmanī*: beyond the mind; *sa śabdaḥ*: that sound; *kṣīṇe*: when it disappears; *akṣare*: in the indestructible; *niḥśabdam*: soundless; *paramam padam*: supreme seat; *yā*: when; *vāsanā*: mental conditioning; *saṃkṣīṇā*: destroyed; *sadā anusaṃdhānāt*: by continual concentration on; *vāyū*: *prāṇa*, vital energy; *manaḥ*: mind; *na saṃśayaḥ*: without doubt; *vilīyete*: becomes absorbed; *nirañjane*: in the pure being; *sahasrāṇi*: thousands; *ca*: and; *śatāni*: hundreds; *bindu*: *bindu*, psychic centre in brain; *koṭi*: points; *yānti layam*: become absorbed; *tatra*: there; *sarve nādake*: in the whole nāda belonging to; *brahma*: brahma, source of existence; *praṇava*: praṇava, primal sound vibration.

Translation

As long as [there is] nāda, [there is] the mind; then, at the end of nāda, [there is] the state beyond the mind. That sound, when it disappears in the indestructible, [becomes] the soundless supreme seat. When mental conditioning [is] destroyed by continual concentration on the nāda, the prāṇa [of] the mind without doubt becomes absorbed in the pure being. Thousands of nāda and hundreds of bindu points become absorbed there in the whole nāda, belonging to Brahma and Praṇava.

Commentary

As long as there is nāda, there is the mind, because it is the mind that perceives the sound. At the end of nāda, there is the state beyond mind, because mind is no longer there to perceive the sound.

Nāda, the subtle vibration that becomes sound, disappears back into the unmanifest dimension, beyond time, space and object. Being beyond any material reality, this dimension is therefore described as indestructible, because there is no objective thing to be destroyed. When the nāda disappears back into the unmanifest, it becomes soundless, because there are no senses, no mind to perceive this subtlest vibration. It is called the supreme seat, because from this soundless vibration the entire creation will be born.

When all the mental conditioning is destroyed, the mind can be transcended. The mind is the link, the go-between the person and the outside world, perceiving and expressing itself in myriad ways, all of which relate with the world and its experiences. However, when the mind is transcended, the person enters the dimension of *brahman*, the pure, luminous and ever-expanding consciousness. The ancient yogis used continual concentration on the nāda as a method of meditation to achieve the elimination of mental conditioning. By this method the prāṇa, or life force, of the mind becomes absorbed in one's pure being, the cosmic consciousness. It is said that in the entire field of nāda there, thousands of nāda, subtle vibrations, and hundreds of bindu, points of light, belonging to brahman and praṇava, are absorbed there. It may be noted that praṇava, the cosmic sound of *Aum*, is the origin of all creation, and bindu, the point of light, the origin of all form.

Verses 51b to 53: Direct path to liberation

सर्वावस्थाविनिर्मुक्तः सर्वचिन्ताविवर्जितः ।।५१।।
मृतवत्तिष्ठते योगी स मुक्तो नात्र संशयः ।
शङ्खदुन्दुभिनादं च न शृणोति कदाचन ।।५२।।
काष्ठवज्जायते देह उन्मन्यावस्थया ध्रुवम् ।
न जानाति स शीतोष्णं न दुःखं न सुखं तथा ।।५३।।

sarvāvasthāvinirmuktaḥ sarvacintāvivarjitaḥ (51b)
mṛtavattiṣṭhate yogī sa mukto nātra saṃśayaḥ
śaṅkhadundubhinādaṃ ca na śṛṇoti kadācana (52)
kāṣṭhavajñāyate deha unmanyāvasthayā dhruvam
na jānāti sa śītoṣṇaṃ na duḥkhaṃ na sukhaṃ tathā (53)

Anvay

vivarjitah: having given up; *sarva cintā*: all thoughts; *vinirmuktaḥ*: freed from; *sarva avasthā*: all states; *yogī*: *yogin*, adept in *yoga*; *tiṣṭhate*: stays still; *mṛtavat*: as if dead; *atra*: at this time; *sa*: he; *na saṃśayaḥ*: without doubt; *muktaḥ*: liberated; *ca*: and; *na kadācana*: never; *śṛṇoti*: he hears; *nādam*: sound; *dundubhi*: large kettle-drum; *śaṅkha*: conch; *dhruvam*: definitely; *unmani avasthayā*: in the state of *unmani*, mind turned inwards; *dehaḥ*: body; *jñāyate*: is felt; *kāṣṭhavat*: like a log; *tathā*: thus; *sa jānāti*: it experiences; *na . . . na*: neither . . . nor; *śīta-uṣṇam*: cold [nor] heat; *duḥkham*: pain; *sukham*: pleasure;

Translation

Having given up all thoughts, freed from all states, the *yogin* stays still as if dead. At this time he [is] without doubt liberated, and he never hears the sound [of] the large kettle-drum [or] conch. Definitely in the state of *unmani*, the body is felt like a log. Thus it experiences neither cold [nor] heat, pain [nor] pleasure.

Commentary

Here, the state of liberation is described. We, who live in modern times, may never experience this heightened state of consciousness, due to our constant involvement with the world and the people around us. We have been conditioned to remain busy all our lives with family, community and professional engagements. This is considered to be a good life, a useful life. Those persons who shun social and professional involvement are considered to be of little worth to themselves and also to others. Although yoga has become very popular around the world, the higher purpose and the path to reach it remains almost entirely unknown.

So now, the seer and teacher of this upaniṣad gives clear instruction on the state of liberation, which was the original aim of yoga from early times. First, the mind must become completely clear and free from all thoughts. Even if a thought arises, there should be no involvement, no response, no reaction, in the mind to that thought. This is the state known as *unmani*, beyond the mind, which can be attained through the practice of meditation, especially nāda yoga. This state of absolute stillness of mind must become established on a daily basis, until it becomes the prevailing mental state and nothing disturbs it.

When absolute stillness of the mind has been established over a long duration of time, the yogi becomes free from all mental states. In this heightened state of consciousness, he remains absolutely silent and unmoving, as if he were dead. At this time, he is liberated without a doubt. He never even hears the inner sounds, which arise as a result of nāda yoga, such as the conch or the large kettle drum. In the state of unmani, the body feels like a log, and it experiences neither heat nor cold, pain nor pleasure, as these are the sensory experiences of the mind.

Verses 54 to 56: Signs of liberation

न मानंनावमानं च संत्यक्त्वा तु समाधिना ।

अवस्थात्रयमन्वेति न चित्तं योगिनः सदा ।।५४।।

जाग्रन्निद्राविनिर्मुक्तः स्वरूपावस्थतामियात् ।।५५।।

दृष्टिः स्थिरा यस्य विनासदृश्यं वायुः स्थिरो यस्य विनाप्रयत्नम् ।

चित्तं स्थिरं यस्य विनावलम्बं स ब्रह्मतारान्तरनादरूप इत्युपनिषत् ।।५६।।

na mānaṃ nāvamānaṃ ca saṃtyaktvā tu samādhinā
avasthātrayamanveti na cittaṃ yoginaḥ sadā (54)
jagrannidrāvinirmuktaḥ svarūpāvasthatāmiyāt (55)
dṛṣṭiḥ sthirā yasya vināsadṛśyaṃ vāyuḥ sthiro yasya vināprayatnam
cittaṃ sthiraṃ yasya vināvalambaṃ sa brahmatārāntaranādarūpa ityupaniṣat (56)

Anvay

cittam: consciousness; *yoginaḥ*: of the *yogin*; *na sadā*: never; *veti*: goes beyond; *trayaman*: third; *avasthā*: state; *samādhinā*: through *samādhi*, final state of meditation; *na . . . na*: without . . . and; *saṃtyaktvā*: giving up; *mānam*: pride; *avamānam*: dishonour; *vinirmuktaḥ*: freed from; *jāgrat*: waking; *nidrā*: sleeping; *iyāt*: he reaches; *svarūpa-avasthatām*: his own natural state; *yasya*: when; *dṛṣṭiḥ*: vision; *sthirā*: fixed; *vinā sadṛśyam*: without that which is visible; *vāyuḥ*: *prāṇa*, vital energy; *sthiraḥ*: still; *vinā prayatnam*: without effort; *cittam*: consciousness; *sthiram*: steady; *vinā avalambam*: without support; *sa*: he; *rūpa*: form; *antara nāda*: inner sound; *brahma*: *Brahma*, source of existence; *tāra*: *Tāra*, Aum; *iti*: declares; *upaniṣat*: Upaniṣad.

Translation

The consciousness of the *yogin* never goes beyond the third state through *samādhi* without giving up pride and dishonour. Freed from waking [and] sleeping, he reaches his own natural state. When the [inner] vision [becomes] fixed without that which is visible, when the *prāṇa* [becomes] still without effort, when consciousness {becomes] steady without support, [then] he [becomes] the form [of] the inner sound [of] *Brahma* [and] *Tāra.* Thus declares the Upaniṣad.

Commentary

The liberated yogi is free from all feeling and expression of pride and shame. Pride is said to be the last vestige of impurity to be overcome on the spiritual journey, and it is the most difficult to remove. The consciousness of the yogi can never go beyond the third level of *samādhi* until pride and shame have been completely eradicated. Samādhi is the highest stage of meditation. It encompasses the state of transcendence, where the individual consciousness merges with the soul, or *ātman.* Ten levels of samādhi have been described in the yoga texts. The first three levels are: 1. *savitarka* (with traces of reasoning or differentiation), *savicara* (with traces of thought in symbolic form) *ānanda* (with bliss).

The description continues that the liberated yogi is neither awake nor asleep to the outside world. This is noted because the body, senses and mind have been transcended in this state. It is as if the awareness has been completely withdrawn from them, and the yogi rests peacefully in the broad expanse of his own consciousness, which is his natural state. Further signs of this state are that the inner vision becomes fixed, without any visible object. The prāṇa becomes still without any effort, which causes the natural rhythm of the breath to cease. The consciousness remains steady and absolutely still, without any support.

When these signs appear, the liberated yogi becomes one with the form of the inner sound of *Brahma* and *Tara*.

ॐ वाङ्मे मनसीति शान्तिः ।।

Om vānme manasīti śāntiḥ

Anvay

iti: let there be; *śāntiḥ*: peace; *manasi*: in mind; *vānme*: in speech.

Translation

Om, let there be peace in mind [and] speech.

इति नादबिन्दूपनिषत्समाप्ता ।

iti: thus; *samāptā*: ends; *upaniṣat*: Upaniṣad.

Thus ends the Upaniṣad.

Appendices

1. Pronunciation Guide

a	nut
ā	father
i	bit
ī	knee
u	hook
ū	sue
ṛ	hurt
e	net
ai	time
o	got
au	house
ṃ	hum
ḥ	h + preceding vowel
k	paprika
kh	ink horn
g	ago
gh	big hut
ṅ	anger
c	chat
ch	much harm
j	jog
jh	raj house
ñ	engine
ṭ	borscht
ṭh	borscht home
ḍ	fresh dill
ḍh	flushed heart
ṇ	rainy
t	tarp
th	scout hall
d	modern
dh	mud hut
n	banal

p	papa
ph	top half
b	maybe
bh	mob hall
m	chroma
y	young
r	merit
l	alas
v	lava
ś	shin
ṣ	sunshine
h	hut

2. **Sanskrit Text**

वैराजात्मोपासानाया संजातज्ञानवह्निना ।
दग्ध्वा कर्मत्रयं योगी यत्पदं याति तद्भजे ।।
ॐ बाङ्मे मनसीति शान्तिः ।।

ॐ अकारो दक्षिणः पक्ष उकारस्तूत्तरः समृतः ।
मकारं पुच्छमित्याहुरर्धमात्रा तु मस्तकम् ।।१।।

पादादिकं गुणाासतासया शरीरं सत्त्वमुच्यते ।
धर्मो ऽस्य दक्षिणं चक्षुरधर्मो ऽथो परः समृतः ।।२।।

भूर्लोकः पादयोस्तस्य भूवर्लोकस्तु जानुनि ।
सुवर्लोकः कटीदेशे नाभिदेशे महर्जगत् ।।३।।
जनोलोकस्तु हृद्देशे कण्ठे लोकस्तपस्ततः ।
भ्रुवोर्ललाटमध्ये तु सत्यलोको व्यवस्थितः ।।४।।

सहस्रार्णमतीवात्र मन्त्र एष प्रदर्शितः ।
एवमेतं समारूधो हंसयोगविचक्षणः ।।५।।
न भिद्यते कर्मचारैः पापकोटिशतैरपि ।६।

आग्नेयी प्रथमा मात्रा वायव्येषा तथापरा ।।६।।
भानुमण्डलसंकाशा भवेन्मात्रा तथोत्तरा ।
परमा चार्धमात्रा या वारुणीं तां विदुर्बुधाः ।।७।।

कालत्रये ऽपि यस्येमा मात्रा नूनं प्रतिष्ठताः ।
एष ओंकार आख्यातो धारणाभिर्निबोधत ।।८।।

घोषिणी प्रथमा मात्रा विद्या मात्रा तथापरा ।
पतङ्गिनी तृतीया स्याच्चतुर्थी वायुवेगिनी ।।९।।
पञ्चमी नामधेया तु षष्टी चैन्द्रीयभिधीयते ।
सप्तमी वैष्णवी नाम अष्टमी शांकरीति च ।।१०।।
नवमी महती नाम धृतिस्तु दशमी मता ।
एकादशी भवेन्नारी ब्राह्मी तु द्वादशी परा ।।११।।

प्रथमायां तु मात्रायां यदि प्राणैर्वियुज्यते ।
भरते वर्षराजासौ सार्वभौमः प्रजायते ।।१२।।

द्वितीयायां समुत्क्रान्तो भवेद्यक्षो महात्मवान् ।
विद्याधरस्तृतीयायां गान्धर्वस्तु चतुर्थिका ।।१३।।

पन्ञम्यामथ मात्रायां यदि प्राणैर्वियुज्यते ।
उषितः सह देवत्वं सोमलोके महीयते ।।१४।।

षष्ठ्यामिन्द्रस्य सायुज्यं सप्तम्यां वैष्णवं पदम् ।
अष्टम्यां व्रज्यते रुद्रं पशूनां च पतिं तथा ।।१५।।

नवम्यां तु महर्लोकं दशम्यां तु जनं व्रजेत् ।
एकादश्यां तपोलोकं द्वादश्यां ब्रह्म शाश्वतम् ।।१६।।

ततः परतरं शुद्धं व्यापकं निर्मलं शिवम् ।
सदोदितं परं ब्रह्म ज्योतिषामुदयो यतः ।।१७।।

अतीन्द्रियं गुणातीतं मनो लीनं यदा भवेत् ।
अनूपमं शिवं शान्तं योगयुक्तं सदाविशेत् ।।१८।।

तद्युक्तस्तन्मयो जन्तुः शनैर्मुञ्चेत्कलेवरम् ।
संस्थितो योगचारेण सर्वसङ्गविवर्जितः ।।१९।।

ततो विलीनपाशोऽसौ विपलः कमलाप्रभुः ।
तेनैव ब्रह्मभावेन परमानन्दमश्नुते ।।२०।।

आत्मानं सततं ज्ञात्वा कालं नय महामते ।
प्रारब्धमखिलं भुञ्जन्नोद्वेगं कर्तुमर्हसि ।।२१।।

उत्पन्ने तत्त्वविज्ञाने प्रारब्धं नैव मुञ्चति ।
तत्त्वज्ञानोदयादूर्ध्वं प्रारब्धं नैव विद्यते ।।२२।।
देहादीनामसत्त्वात्तु यथा स्वप्ने विबोधतः ।२३।

कर्म जन्मान्तरीयं यत्प्रारब्धमिति कीर्तितम् ।।२३।।
तत्तु जन्मान्तराभावात्पुंसो नैवास्ति कर्हिचित ।२४।

स्वप्नदेहो यथाध्यस्तस्तथैवायं हि देहकः ।।२४।।
अध्यस्तस्य कुतो जन्म जन्माभावे कुतः स्थितिः ।२५।

उपादानं प्रपञ्चस्य मृद्भाण्डस्येव पश्यति ।।२५।।
अज्ञानं चेति वेदान्तैस्तस्मिन्नष्टे क्व विश्वता ।२६।

यथा रज्जुं परित्यज्य सर्पं गृह्णाति वै भ्रमात् ।।२६।।
तद्वत्सत्यमविज्ञाय जगत्पश्यति मूढधीः ।
रज्जुखण्डे परिज्ञाते सर्परूपं न तिष्ठति ।।२७।।

अधिष्ठाने तथा ज्ञाते प्रपञ्चे शून्यतां गते ।
देहस्यापि प्रपञ्चत्वात्प्रारब्धावस्थितिः कुतः ।।२८।।
अज्ञानजनबोधार्थं प्रारब्धमिति चोच्यते ।२९।

ततः कालवशादेव प्रारब्धे तु क्षयं गते ।।२९।।
ब्रह्मप्रणवसंधानो नादो ज्योतिर्मयः शिवः ।
स्वयमाविर्भवेदात्मा मेघापाये ऽशुमानिव ।।३०।।

सिद्धासने स्थितो योगी मुद्रां संधाय वैष्णवीं ।
शृणुयाद्दक्षिणे कर्णे नादमन्तर्गतं सदा ।।३१।।

अभ्यस्यमानो नादो ऽयं बाह्यमावृणुते ध्वनिः ।
पक्षाद्विपक्षमखिलं जित्वा तुर्यपदंव्रजेत् ।।३२।।

श्रूयते प्रथमाभ्यासे नादो नानाविधो महान् ।
वर्धमाने तथाभ्यासे श्रूयते सूक्ष्मसूक्ष्मतः ।।३३।।
आदौ जलधिजीमूतभेरीनिर्झरसंभवः ।
मध्ये मर्दलशब्दाभो घण्टाकाहलजस्तथा ।।३४।।

अन्ते तु किंकिणीवंशवीणाभ्रमरनिस्वनः ।
इति नानाविधा नादाः श्रूयन्ते सूक्ष्मसूक्ष्मतः ।।३५।।

महति श्रूयमाणे तु महाभेर्यादिकध्वनौ ।
तत्र सूक्ष्मं सूक्ष्मतरं नादमेव परामृशेत् ।।३६।।

घनमुत्सृज्य वा सूक्ष्मे सूक्ष्ममुत्सृज्य वा घने ।
रममाणमपि क्षिप्तं मनो नान्यत्र चालयेत् ।।३७।।
यत्र कुत्रापि वा नादे लगति प्रथमं मनः ।
तत्र तत्र स्थिरीभूत्वा तेन सार्धं विलीयते ।।३८।।

विस्मृत्य सकलं बाह्यं नादे दुग्धाम्बुवन्मनः ।
एकीभूयाथ सहसा चिदाकाशे विलीयते ।।३९।।

उदासीनस्ततो भूत्वा सदाभ्यासेन सम्यमी ।
उन्मनीकारकं सद्यो नादमेवावधारयेत् ।।४०।।

सर्वचिन्तां समुत्सृज्य सर्व चेष्टाविवर्जितः ।
नादमेवानुसंदध्यान्नादे चित्तं विलीयते ।।४१।।

मकरन्दं पिबन्भृङ्गो गन्धान्नापेक्षते यथा ।
नादासक्तं सदा चित्तं विषयं न हि काङ्क्षति ।।४२।।
बद्धः सुनादगन्धेन सद्यः संत्यक्तचापलः ।४३।

नादग्रहणतश्चित्तमन्तरङ्गभुजङ्गमः ।।४३।।

विस्मृत्य विश्वमेकाग्रः कुत्रचिन्न हि धावति ।४४।

मनोमत्तगजेन्द्रस्य विषयोद्यानचारिनः ।।४४।।
नियामनसमर्थो ऽयं निनादो मिशिताङ्कुशः ।
नादो ऽन्तरङ्गसारङ्गबन्धने वागुरायते ।।४५।।
अन्तरङ्गसमुद्रस्य रोधे वेलायते ऽपि वा ।४६।

ब्रह्मप्रणवसंलग्ननादो ज्योतिर्मयात्मकः ।।४६।।
मनस्तत्र लयं याति तद्विष्णोः परं पदम् ।४७।

तावदाकाशसंकल्पो यावच्छब्दः प्रवर्तते ।।४७।।
निःशब्दं तत्परं ब्रह्म परमात्मा समीयते ।४८।

नादो यावन्मनस्तावन्नादान्ते ऽपि मनोन्मनी ।।४८।।
सशब्दश्चाक्षरे क्षीणे निःशब्दं परमं पदं
सदा नादानुसंधानात्संक्षीणा वासना तु या ।।४९।।
निरञ्जने विलीयेते मनोवायू न संशयः
नादकोटिसहस्राणि बिन्दुकोटिशतानि च ।।५०।।
सर्वे तत्र लयं यान्ति ब्रह्मप्रवनादके ।५१।

सर्वावस्थाविनिर्मुक्तः सर्वचिन्ताविवर्जितः ।।५१।।
मृतवत्तिष्ठते योगी स मुक्तो नात्र संशयः ।
शङ्खदुन्दुभिनादं च न शृणोति कदाचन ।।५२।।
काष्ठवज्ज्ञायते देह उन्मन्यावस्थया ध्रवम् ।
न जानाति स शीतोष्णं न दुःखं न सुखं तथा ।।५३।।

न मानंनावमानं च संत्यक्त्वा तु समाधिना ।
अवस्थात्रयमन्वेति न चित्तं योगिनः सदा ।।५४।।
जाग्रन्निद्राविनिर्मुक्तः स्वरूपावस्थतामियात् ।।५५।।
दृष्टिः स्थिरा यस्य विनासदृश्यं वायुः स्थिरो यस्य विनाप्रयत्नम् ।
चित्तं स्थिरं यस्य विनावलम्बं स ब्रह्मतारान्तरनादरूप इत्युपनिषत् ।।५६।।

ॐ वाङ्मे मनसीति शान्तिः ।।

इति नादबिन्दूपनिषत्समाप्ता

3. Continuous Translation

Opening Invocation

Having burned the three *karmas* through the fire of knowledge, born through devotion to the self, [who is] derived from Virāj, the yogin goes to that seat where he worships.

Om, let there be peace in speech and mind.

1.

The sound 'a' is declared [to be] the right wing [of] AUM, 'u' the left, 'm' the tail, and the half-syllable is said [to be] the head.

2.

It is said the *guṇas* start at the feet, *sattvam* is its body; *dharma*, it is declared, is its right eye, and *adharma* its other [eye].

3 and 4.

The *bhūrloka* [is] in its feet, the *bhūvarloka* in its knees; *suvarloka* in the region [of] the hips; *maharjagat* in the region [of] the navel. *Janoloka* is located in the region [of] the heart; from there *tapoloka* in the throat, and *satyaloka* in the centre [of] the forehead [between] the eyebrows.

5 and 6a.

The flowing *mantra* is explained here as a thousand-waved intelligence. One who is proficient [in] *yoga*, having thus mounted the *haṃsa*, is not affected by the bonds of *karma* or even by a hundred crores [of] sins.

6b and 7.

The first *mātrā* relates to Agni, the second to Vāyu, then the next is bright [like] the orb [of] the sun, and the last [is] the supreme *ardhamātrā*; this the wise know relates to Vāruṇa.

8.
Now the *mātrās* of each are also formed of three parts. This is called the *oṃkāra*. You can know [it] through the *dhāraṇās*.

9 to 11.
The first is Ghoṣiṇī, then the next Vidyā, the third Pataṅginī, the fourth Vāyuveginī, the fifth Nāmadheyā; and the sixth is called Śiva, the seventh Vaiṣṇavī, the eighth's name is said [to be] Śāṃkarī, the ninth Mahatī, the tenth is regarded as Dhṛti, the eleventh is Nārī, then the twelfth [is]
the Supreme Reality.

12.
Now, if he is separated from the *prāṇas* (i.e. dies) in the first *mātrā,* he is reborn [as] a universal monarch in *Bharatavarṣa* (India).

13.
Having passed away in the second, he becomes a great *yakṣa*; in the third a *vidyādhara*; and in the fourth a *gāndharva*.

14.
Then, if he is separated from the prāṇas in the fifth, he lives in the world [of] the moon as exalted as a *deva.*

15.
[If] in the sixth, [he is in] communion with Indra; in the seventh, he reaches the seat of Vishnu, and then, in the eighth, Rudra, lord of [all] creatures.

16.
[If] in the ninth, he reaches, *mahaloka*; and in the tenth, *janoloka*; in the eleventh, *tapoloka*; in the twelfth, everlasting Brahma.

17.
The supreme consciousness, which rises from light, is always declared [to be] Śiva [who is] beyond these [*mātrās*], pure, all-pervading [and] resplendent.

18.
When the mind is absorbed beyond the *indriyas* [and] the *guṇas*, [then], always immersed in yoga, he should enter the incomparable auspicious Śiva.

19.
The person [who is] established [there and] absorbed in it, should slowly relinquish support, intent upon the observance of yoga, avoiding all company.

20.
Then, the instant that person is freed from the bonds [of] riches [and] marriage, he thus attains supreme bliss by absorption in Brahma.

21.
O Intelligent One, spend your time continually knowing the self, enjoying [your] entire *prārabdha*, without trying to resist [it].

22 and 23a.
Even when knowledge of the *tattvas* has emerged, prārabdha does not leave [him], but he is not affected by prārabdha [after] the rising up [of] *tattvajñāna*, because of the unreal nature of the body and other [material things], as if perceived in a dream.

23b and 24a.
That *karma* associated with former births is called *prārabdha.* Yet the person who has no rebirth never experiences it.

24b and 25a.
As the body in a dream [is] illusory, so indeed [is] this body. Where [is] the birth of that [which is] illusory? Where does it exist in the absence of rebirth?

25b and 26a.
He sees, in accordance with Vedānta, [that] *ajñāna* [is] the material cause of the form of the clay-pot, and asks, if *ajñāna* is no more, where then [is] the universe?

26b and 27.
Just as he considers from a distance a rope [to be] a snake, in the same way, not knowing the truth,
the fool sees the world [as] separate from Brahma. When he recognises [it] as a piece [of] rope, the appearance [of] a snake does not remain.

28 and 29a.
Thus, when he knows emptiness, when the material support has gone, where [is] the abode [of] prārabdha, as the body is also of the phenomenal world. And so it is said prārabdha [is] for the purpose of teaching those born in *ajñāna.*

29b and 30.
Then, in the course of time, when *prārabdha* have come to an end, the *ātman*, [which is] the auspicious sound consisting of light [and] uniting *praṇava* [with] *brahma*, quickly reveals itself, like [the sun] when the clouds disperse.

31.
The yogin, seated in *siddhāsana*, having adopted the *vishnu mudrā*, hears the *nāda* [which] always goes into the right ear.

32.

This sound, [whose] inner tone [is] the aim of the practice, is hidden from the outer. Having conquered all obstacles, he enters the fourth state in fifteen days.

33 to 35.
At the beginning of his practice he hears many loud sounds; then, as his practice increases, he hears [them as] more subtle, [until] scarcely audible. At first the source [of the sounds seems to be from] the ocean, clouds, kettle-drums [and] waterfalls; then, in the middle [stage], [they are] like sounds caused by drums, bells [and] horns. At the last stage [there are] sounds [of] small bells, flutes, lutes [and] bees. Thus various sounds are heard, [becoming] more and more subtle.

36.
When at first the loud sound [of] the great drum is heard, then he should just concentrate on its most subtle sounds.

37 and 38.
Either leaving the gross sound for the subtle, or leaving the subtle sound for the gross, even while delighting [in them], the mind [becomes] distracted, [and so] should not be moved to other [sounds]. Or whichever sound the mind first attaches itself to, securely fixed there, it becomes absorbed in it.

39.
Having forgotten all external [experiences], the mind, uniting with the sound [as] milk [with] water, is immediately absorbed in *cidākāśa*.

40.
Then, having become indifferent to passion by the continual practice [of] self-control, he should at once give his full attention to the inner sound.

41.

Having abandoned every thought and renounced every desire, he should place all his attention on the inner sound, until his consciousness becomes absorbed in it.

42 and 43a.
Just as the bee drinking the nectar is not concerned with its fragrance, so the consciousness, always intent on the nāda, does not crave sensual enjoyment [as it is] bound by the nāda's own sweet fragrance, its fickle nature relinquished.

43b and 44a.
The inner serpent [of] consciousness [which] holds the *nāda*, concentrating [on it], unaware of all [else], does not rush here and there.

44b to 46a.
This sound [is] a sharp hook, suitable for restraining the mind [which is] like a mad elephant roaming the pleasure garden [of] sensual enjoyment. The nāda ensnares as a fetter [for] the inner deer, or is also a shore, which holds back the inner ocean.

46b to 47a.
The nāda, arising from *Praṇava* [and] *Brahma*, has the nature of light. There the mind becomes absorbed. This [is] the supreme seat of Viṣṇu.

47b to 48a.
As long as sound is produced, then [there is] the will of *ākāśa*. Then the supreme self is equal to the soundless supreme Brahma.

48b to 51a.
As long as [there is] nāda, [there is] the mind; then, at the end of nāda, [there is] the state beyond the mind. That sound, when it disappears in the indestructible, [becomes] the

soundless supreme seat. When mental conditioning [is] destroyed by continual concentration on the nāda, the prāṇa [of] the mind without doubt becomes absorbed in the pure being. Thousands of nāda and hundreds of bindu points become absorbed there in the whole nāda, belonging to Brahma and Praṇava.

51b to 53.
Having given up all thoughts, freed from all states, the *yogin* stays still as if dead. At this time he [is] without doubt liberated, and he never hears the sound [of] the large kettle-drum [or] conch. Definitely in the state of *unmani*, the body is felt like a log. Thus it experiences neither cold [nor] heat, pain [nor] pleasure.

54 to 56.
The consciousness of the *yogin* never goes beyond the third state through *samādhi* without giving up pride and dishonour. Freed from waking [and] sleeping, he reaches his own natural state. When the [inner] vision [becomes] fixed without that which is visible, when the *prāṇa* [becomes] still without effort, when consciousness {becomes] steady without support, [then] he [becomes] the form [of] the inner sound [of] *Brahma* [and] *Tāra.* Thus declares the Upaniṣad.

Om, let there be peace in mind [and] speech.

Thus ends the Upaniṣad.

ध्यानबिन्दूपनिषत्

dhyānabindūpaniṣat

Meditation Point Upaniṣad

Opening Invocation

ध्यात्वा यद्ब्रह्ममात्रं ते स्वावशेषधिया ययुः ।
योगतत्त्वज्ञानफलं तत्स्वमात्रं विचिन्तये ।।
ॐ सह नाववत्विति शान्तिः ।।

dhyātvā yadbrahmamātraṃ te svāvaśeṣadhiyā yayuḥ
yogatattvajñānaphalaṃ tatsvamātraṃ vicintaye
om saha nāvavatviti śāntiḥ

Anvay

dhyātvā: having meditated on; *brahma-mātraṃ*: totality of Brahman; *sva-avaśeṣa*: own remainder; *dhiyā*: by thought, mentally; *yayuḥ*: swiftly; *vicintaye*: I reflect on; *sva-mātraṃ*: own totality; *yoga-tattva-jñāna-phalam*: fruit of knowledge of the essence of yoga; *iti*: saying; *avavatu*: may this benefit; *nau*: both of us; *saha*: together; *śāntiḥ*: peace.

Translation

Having meditated on the totality of Brahman, I reflect mentally on the remainder of my own totality, the fruit of knowledge, the essence of yoga, saying Om, may this [teaching] benefit both of us together. Peace.

Commentary

This invocation expresses the connection of the *Riṣi*, or seer, of this upaniṣad with the ever illumined state of consciousness, the totality of *Brahman*, through meditation. He has further contemplated on his own individual consciousness, and realised the essence of yoga, which is the fruit of knowledge. Thus, he says, 'may this teaching benefit both of us together', meaning may the disciple and the teacher both be uplifted through this knowledge.

Verse 1: Dhyāna yoga destroys sin

यदि शैलसं पापं विस्तीर्णं बहुयोजनम् ।

भिद्यते ध्यानयोगेन नान्यो भेदः कदाचन ।।१।।

yadi śailasaṃ pāpaṃ vistīrṇaṃ bahuyojanam
bhidyate dhyānayogena nānyo bhedaḥ kadācana (1)

Anvay

yadi: even if; *pāpam*: sin; *vistīrṇam*: extends; *śailasam*: mountain; *bahu-yojanam*: many *yojanas* (one *yojana* is approximately 9 miles); *bhidyate*: it is destroyed; *dhyāna-yoga*: *yoga* of meditation; *na kadācana*: never; *anyaḥ bhedaḥ*: another destroyer.

Translation

Even if sin extends [like] a mountain [for] many *yojanas*, it is destroyed by *dhyānayoga*; [there has] never [been] another destroyer.

Commentary

The word 'sin' equates with negative action, which is wrong and which does harm to oneself and/or others. Another word for action is *karma*. Action is begotten from the mind and all actions are stored in the mind for further use and association. Not a single action that one does goes away. although certain actions may be forgotten, all remain in the deeper recesses of the subconscious mind lifelong. Even at the time of death, the actions are bundled into what is called a 'karmic sheath', which passes on together with the soul. In this sense, every person is bound by his or her actions. If the actions are positive and beneficial, the results will be auspicious and harmonious. If the actions are evil and harmful, the results will be painful and unpleasant.

All human beings are a mixed bag of good and bad karmas. Some carry more or less karmas than others. Some carry more good karmas and others carry more bad. We are born on Earth in order to fulfil and finish our karmas. The good karmas that one carries bear no stigma and do no harm. Therefore, they can be left until last. However, the bad karmas, especially those which are ripening and must be fulfilled in this lifetime, carry much pain, difficulty, and trauma. These bad karmas, or sins, must be removed from the mind and consciousness in a way that does not promote further pain and distress to oneself and to others. If one goes on reenacting them over and over, there will be great distress to others, as well as to oneself. One can see this in habitual bouts of anger or abusive behaviour.

If one does not vent the negativity one feels from inside, through harsh speech or action, then what is one to do with it? How is one to deal with it? Here, in the first verse of this teaching, it says that, even if one's sin or negativity extends like a mountain that is many miles high, it can all be eliminated through the practice of *dhyāna yoga*, the yoga of meditation. And there has never been another way to destroy it.

Verse 2: Bindu nāda

बीजाक्षरं परं बिन्दुं नादं तस्योपरि स्थितम् ।
सशब्दं चाक्षरे क्षीणे निःशब्दं परं पदम् ।।२।।

bījākṣaraṃ paraṃ binduṃ nādaṃ tasyopari sthitam
saśabdaṃ cākṣare kṣīne niḥśabdaṃ paraṃ padam (2)

Anvay

nāda: inner most subtle sound; *sthitam*: is; *upari*: above; *bīja-akṣara*: seed letter containing latent power of sound; *param bindum*: supreme point; *sa śabdaḥ*: that sound; *kṣīne*: when it disappears; *akṣare*: in the indestructible; *niḥśabdam*: soundless; *paramam padam*: supreme seat.

Translation

The *nāda* is above the *bīja akṣara*, the supreme point. That sound, when it disappears in the indestructible, [becomes] the soundless supreme seat.

Commentary

At bindu cakra, the energy centre located at the top back of the head, the *nāda* is located above the *bīja akṣara,* the seed letter of that centre, containing the latent power of sound. The word *bindu* means 'point'. This is the point where the unmanifest reality enters the manifest. Hence, it is the source of all creation and manifestation. At bindu cakra the inner nāda, or subtle most sound, is born and it rests just above the bīja akṣara, at the supreme point. Similarly, at the time of dissolution, that subtle most sound disappears back into the unmanifest, the indestructible, where it becomes the soundless supreme seat.

Verse 3: Highest stage of nāda yoga

अनाहतं तु यच्छब्दं तस्य शब्दस्य यत्परं ।
तत्परं बिन्दते यस्तु स योगी छिन्नसंशयः ॥३॥

anāhataṃ tu yacchabdaṃ tasya śabdasya yatparam
tatparaṃ bindate yastu sa yogī chinnasaṃśayaḥ (3)

Anvay

sa yogī: that *yogin*; *yaḥ*: in whom; *param śabdam*: highest sound; *tasya śabdasya*: of that sound; *bindate*: is no more; *chinna*: has lost; *saṃśayaḥ*: doubt; *anāhatam*: unstruck sound; *param*: highest.

Translation

That yogin, in whom the highest sound of that sound is no more, has lost [all] doubt [that] the soundless sound [is] the highest [stage of *nāda yoga*].

Commentary

Nāda yoga begins as a practice of concentration, where the yogi follows the various sounds, one by one, gradually refining his perception as the sounds become more and more subtle. In this way the awareness is led by sound itself from the external gross plane to the interior subtle plane. With mastery of the practice, the mind is transcended and the awareness is merged in the highest, supreme sound. Ultimately, even the highest sound is no more. That yogi, in whom the subtlest vibration of that supreme sound is heard no more, realises beyond a doubt that the soundless sound is the highest stage of nāda yoga.

Verse 4: Power of the supreme nāda

वालाग्रशतसाहस्रं तस्य भागस्य भागिनः ।
तस्य भागस्य भागार्धं तत्क्षये तु निरञ्जनम् ।।४।।

vālāgraśatasāhasraṃ tasya bhāgasya bhāginaḥ
tasya bhāgasya bhāgārdhaṃ tatkṣaye tu nirañjanam (4)

Anvay

agra: point; *vāla*: hair; *bhāgasya*: if . . is divided into; *śata-sāhasram*: one hundred thousand; *bhāginaḥ*: participant, i.e. *nāda*; *bhāgasya*: if . . is divided into; *ardham*: half; *bhāga*: division; *tu*: then; *tat kṣaye*: when this is absorbed; *nirañjanam*: pure.

Translation

If the point [of] a hair is divided into one hundred thousand [parts], [and] if this *nāda* is divided into half of [each] division, then when this is absorbed, [the *yogin* attains] the pure [state].

Commentary

The supreme nāda is the source and the first cause of creation. The power of this vibration is so great that it is impossible to measure or describe. So, an analogy is given here that if the point of a hair were split into 100,000 parts, and if this supreme sound were divided into half of each part, then when it is absorbed, the nāda yogi attains the stainless, liberated state.

Verses 5 to 7: Knowledge of Brahman

पुष्पमध्ये यथा गन्धः पयोमध्ये यथा घृतम् ।
तिलमध्ये यथा तैलं पापाणेष्विव काञ्चनम् ।।५।।
एवं सर्वाणि भूतानि मणौ सूत्र इवात्मनि ।
स्थिरबुद्धिरसंसूढो ब्रह्मविद्ब्रह्मणि स्थितः ।।६।।
तिलानां तु यथा तैलं पुष्पे गन्ध इवाश्रितः ।
पुरुषस्य शरीरे तु सबाह्याभ्यन्तरे स्थितः ।।७।।

puṣpamadhya yathā gandhaḥ payomadhye yathā ghṛtam
tilamadhye yathā tailaṃ pāpāṇeṣviva kāñcanam (5)
evaṃ sarvāni bhūtāni manau sūtra iyātmani
sthirabuddhirasaṃsūdho brahmavidbrahmani sthitaḥ (6)
tilānāṃ tu yathā tailaṃ puṣpe gandha ivāśritaḥ
puruṣasya śarīre tu sabāhyābhyantare sthitaḥ (7)

Anvay

yathā: just as; *gandhaḥ*: fragrance; *puṣpa-madhye*: in flowers; *ghṛtam*: ghee; *payo-madhye*: in milk; *tailam*: oil; *tila-madhye*: in sesame; *kāñcanam*: gold; *pāpāṇeṣu*: in rocks; *evam*: thus; *brahmavid*: one who knows the Vedas; *sthitaḥ*: is established; *brahmani*: in Brahman; *sūdhaḥ*: having rejected; *rasam*: sensual pleasure; *sthira buddhi*: stable mind; *sarvāni bhūtāni*: all creatures; *iva*: like; *sūtra*: string; *manau*: pearls; *ātmani*: in the self; *tu*: so; *yathā*: just as; *tailam*: oil; *āśritaḥ*: is dependent; *tilānām*: on the sesame; *iva*: and; *gandhaḥ*: fragrance; *puṣpe*: on the flower; *tu*: so; *puruṣasya*: *puruṣa*; *sthitaḥ*: does exist; *śarīre*: in the body; *sabāhya*: outside; *ābhyantare*: inside.

Translation

Just as fragrance [is] in flowers, ghee in milk, oil in sesame, gold in rocks, thus one who knows the Vedas is established in Brahman, having rejected sensual pleasure [and being of] stable mind, [sees] all creatures, like a string [of] pearls, in the self. So just as the oil is dependent on the sesame and fragrance on the flower, so does *puruṣa* exist in the body, [both] outside [and] inside.

Commentary

The vedas are the ancient knowledge, which were revealed to the rishis and seers of the *Aryan* culture from early times. They are the bedrock of all the philosophies, teachings, sects and religions that have arisen on the Indian sub-continent over millennia, and have an important influence on the culture and way of life, even today. Just as the prominent religions of this time speak of God, Allah, Jehovah, the vedas speak of Brahman, the one universal, ever-luminous and expanding consciousness. The ultimate objective of yoga, and of all spiritual practice from early times, was to merge the individual, limited consciousness with the unlimited, universal consciousness of Brahman.

These verses explain the presence of Brahman, the One consciousness, which is everywhere and in everything, in a simple and beautiful way. Just as fragrance is inherent in flowers, as ghee (clarified butter) is processed from milk, as oil is a part of the sesame seed, as gold is found in rocks, in the same way, Brahman is established in the vedas. Therefore, one who knows the vedas is established in Brahman. We must consider that knowing the vedas was not achieved simply by reading them. This knowledge had to be studied under the tutelage of a master teacher, memorised, sung and finally meditated upon. So, it is said that one who knows the vedas becomes established in Brahman.

Being established in Brahman really means to realise one's highest conscious potential, and to remain in this elevated state for long durations of time. It is not simply a random experience that may or may not come and go. Brahman is a permanent and true reality, which permeates the perception of those who have studied the vedas, disciplined their senses and lead a meditative lifestyle. By rejecting sensual pleasure, the mind becomes steady and capable of penetrating the inner depths of consciousness. Such a person perceives the self and all of existence through the light of this alternate state. He sees that all beings are interconnected, like a string of pearls, in the light of consciousness. Hence, just as the oil is dependent on the sesame seed, and the fragrance on the flower, similarly, *puruṣa*, the consciousness, exists within the body and outside everywhere and in everything, as well.

Verse 8: Self is both manifest and unmanifest

वृक्षं तु सकलं विद्याच्छाया तस्यैव निष्कला ।
सकले निष्कले भावे सर्वत्रात्मा व्यवस्थितः ।।८।।

vṛkṣaṃ tu sakalaṃ vidyācchāyā tasyaiva niṣkalā
sakale niṣkale bhāve sarvatrātmā vyavasthitaḥ (8)

Anvay

tu: now; *vidyāt*: knows; *vṛkṣam*: tree; *sakalam*: with parts; *tasya chāyā*: its shadow; *niṣkalā*: without parts; *ātmā*: Self; *vyavasthitaḥ*: exists; *sarvatra*: everywhere; *bhāve*: in the state; *sakale*: with parts; *niṣkale*: without parts.

Translation

Now [the *yogin*] knows the tree with parts [and] its shadow without parts [and that] the Self exists everywhere, in the state with parts [and] without parts.

Commentary

The tree with parts refers to the manifest dimension of existence; while its shadow, which is without parts, represents the unmanifest. Together the manifest and the unmanifest make up the entire existence. The manifest is an evolute of the unmanifest. In the absence of the unmanifest, the manifest cannot be born or evolve. The unmanifest supports and sustains the manifest at all times and in all aspects. The yogi is aware of this relationship between the manifest and the unmanifest,

and the purpose of his practice is to merge his manifest being with the unmanifest. In this sense, the body, mind, senses and ego all relate with the manifest being. The consciousness, the ātman, the self, the spirit relate with the unmanifest.

Although all beings are rooted in the unmanifest, most have forgotten their origin, and identify completely with the manifest. This becomes a major source of pain, anxiety, and stress, because everything in the material world is impermanent. Everyone who is born on the manifest plane lives in the body for only a designated number of years, and then passes back into the the unmanifest. In this way the souls come and go, entering bodies for a short lifetime, dropping the bodies and returning to their origin. The yogi is a person who strives to remember his origin, and to live his life on Earth with that awareness. Thus he knows that the self, the consciousness, exists everywhere on the manifest plane, in the state with division and parts, and on the unmanifest, which is undivided, without parts, as well.

Verse 9a: Meditation on Om

ओमित्येकाक्षरं ब्रह्म ध्येयं सर्वमुमुक्षुभिः ।९।

omityekākṣaraṃ brahma dhyeyaṃ sarvamumukṣubhiḥ (9a)

Anvay

iti: it is declared; *eka akṣaram om*: one imperishable sound *Om*; *dhyeyam*: should be contemplated on; *brahma*: as Brahman; *sarva-mumukṣubhiḥ*: by all who desire liberation.

Translation

It is declared the one imperishable sound *Om* should be contemplated on as Brahman by all who desire liberation.

Commentary

Om is said to be the one imperishable sound, because it is the first sound that ushered the manifest creation into existence from the unmanifest. *Om* should be meditated upon because it is the source of all manifest existence, and the way back to the unmanifest. Visualisation of the letter *Om*, or repetition of the sound in any manner, whether sung or chanted aloud, whispered, intoned mentally or repeated with the heartbeat or the breath, calms the mind and brings the awareness to the undivided space of consciousness. By continuous repetition or visualisation of *Om* over many years, the yogi is able to delve deeper and deeper into the unmanifest consciousness, and discover his eternal self. Therefore, the sound of *Om* should be meditated upon as Brahman, the one ever-expanding universal consciousness, by all those who desire liberation from the bondage of worldly existence.

Verses 9b to 13a: Three components of Om

पृथिव्यग्निश्च ऋग्वेदो भूरित्येव पितामहः ।।९।।

अकारे तु लयं प्राप्ते प्रथमे प्रणवांशके ।

अन्तरिक्षं यजुर्वायुर्भुवो विष्णुर्जनार्दनः ।।१०।।

उकारे तु लयं प्राप्ते द्वितीये प्रणवांशके ।

द्यौः सूर्यः सामवेदश्च स्वरित्येव महेश्वरः ।।११।।

मकारे तु लयं प्राप्ते तृतीये प्रणवांशके ।

अकारः पीतवर्णः स्याद्रजोगुण उदीरितः ।।१२।।

उकारः सात्त्विकः शुक्लो मकारः कृष्णतामसः ।१३।

pṛthivyagniśca ṛgvedo bhūrityeva pitāmahaḥ (9b)
akāre tu layaṃ prāpte prathame praṇavāṃśake
antarikṣaṃ yajurvāyurbhuvo viṣṇurjanārdanaḥ (10)
ukāre tu layaṃ prāpte dvitīye praṇavāṃśake
dyauḥ sūryaḥ sāmavedaśca svarityeva maheśvaraḥ (11)
makāre tu layaṃ prāpte tṛtīye praṇavāṃśake
akāraḥ pītavarṇaḥ syādrajoguṇa udīritaḥ (12b)
ukāraḥ sāttvikaḥ śuklo makāraḥ kṛṣṇatāmasaḥ (13a)

Anvay

pṛthivī: *Pṛthivī*, earth element; *agni*: *Agni*, fire element; *ṛgveda*: *Rigveda*, ancient sacred Vedic text; *bhūḥ*: *Bhūḥ*, plane of earthly existence; *eva*: and; *pitāmahaḥ*: Brahma, father of all; *layam*: are absorbed; *akāre*: when the sound 'A'; *prathame aṃśake*: first part; *praṇava*: *praṇava*, AUM; *prāpte*: is attained; *antarikṣam*: region between heaven and earth; *yajuḥ*: knowledge of sacrifice; *vāyuḥ*: air element; *bhuvaḥ*: astral plane; *viṣṇuḥ*: Viṣṇu; *janārdanaḥ*: harasser of men; *layam*: are absorbed; *ukāre*: when the sound 'U'; *dvitīye aṃśake*: second part; *praṇava*: *praṇava*, AUM; *prāpte*: is attained; *dyauḥ*: sky; *sūryaḥ*: sun; *svariti*: sounds;

sāmavedaḥ: Sāmaveda, Veda of Chants; *ca eva*: and even; *maheśvaraḥ*: Great Lord Śiva; *layam*: are absorbed; *makāre*: when the sound 'M'; *tṛtīye aṃśake*: third part; *praṇava*: *praṇava*, AUM; *prāpte*: is attained; *akāraḥ*: letter 'A'; *pīta-varṇaḥ*: yellow [in] colour; *udīritaḥ syāt*: is said to be; *rajoguṇa*: rajasic; *ukāraḥ*: letter 'U'; *śuklaḥ*: white; *sāttvikaḥ*: sattvic; *makāraḥ*: letter 'M'; *kṛṣṇa*: black; *tāmasaḥ*: tamasic.

Translation

Pṛthivī, Agni, Rigveda, Bhūḥ and Brahma are absorbed when the sound 'A', the first part [of] *praṇava*, is attained. The region between heaven and earth, knowledge of sacrifice, air element, astral plane [and] Vishnu, harasser of men are [all] absorbed when the sound 'U', the second part [of] *praṇava*, is attained. The sky, sun, sounds [of] the Sāmaveda and even the Great Lord Śiva are [all] absorbed when the sound 'M', the third part [of] *praṇava*, is attained. The letter 'A' [is] yellow [in] colour [and] is said to be rajasic. The letter 'U' [is] white [and] sattvic. The letter 'M' [is] black [and] tamasic.

Verses 13b to 15: Qualities of a Brahman

अष्टाङ्ग च चतुष्पादं त्रिस्थानं पञ्चदैवतम् ।।१३।।

ओंकार यो न जानाति ब्रह्मणो न भवेत्तु सः

प्रणवो धनुः शरो ह्यात्मा ब्रह्म तल्लक्ष्यमुच्यते ।।१४।।

अप्रमत्तेन वेद्धव्यं शरवत्तन्मयो भवेत् ।

निवर्तन्ते क्रियाः सर्वास्तस्मिन्दृष्टे परावरे ।।१५।।

aṣṭāṅga ca catuṣpādaṃ tristhānaṃ pañcadaivatam (13b)
omkāra yo na jānāti brahmano na bhavettu saḥ
praṇavo dhanuḥ śaro hyātmā brahma tallakṣyamucyate (14b)
apramattena veddhavyaṃ śaravattanmayo bhavet
nivartante kriyāḥ sarvāstasmindṛṣṭe parāvare (15)

Anvay

saḥ yaḥ: he who; *na jānāti*: does not know; *omkāra*: *Omkāra*, sound of Om; *aṣṭa-aṅga*: eight parts; *catur-pādam*: four feet; *tri-sthānam*: three states; *ca*: and; *pañca-daivatam*: five deities; *na bhavet*: is not; *brahmana*: Brahman; *ucyate*: it is said; *hi*: thus; *praṇava*: *praṇava,* Om; *ātmā*: *ātmā,* Self; *brahma*: *Brahma,* Highest Reality; *lakṣyam*: aim; *veddhavyam*: aiming; *apramattena*: carefully; *śaravat*: like the arrow; *bhavet*: becomes; *tat mayaḥ*: one with it; *parāvare*: when the totality; *tasmin*: of this; *dṛṣṭe*: is seen; *nivartante*: it reverses; *sarvāḥ kriyāḥ*: all actions.

Translation

He who does not know *Omkāra* [as having] eight parts, four feet, three states and five deities is not a Brahman. It is said thus: *praṇava* is the bow, *ātmā* the arrow, *brahma* the aim. Aiming carefully, he, like the arrow, becomes one with it. When the totality of this is seen, it reverses all actions.

Verses 16 to 19: The Power of Oṃkāra

ओंकारप्रभवा देवा ओंकारप्रभवाः स्वराः ।
ओंकारप्रभवं सर्वं त्रैलोक्यं सचराचरम् ।।१६।।
ह्रस्वो दहति पापानि दीर्घः संपत्प्रदो ऽव्ययः ।
अर्धमात्रासमा युक्तः प्रणवो मोक्षदातक्तः ।।१७।।
तैलधारामिवाच्छिन्नं दीर्घघण्टानिनादवत् ।
अवाच्यं प्रणवस्याग्रं यस्तं वेद स वेदवित् ।।१८।।
हृत्पद्मकर्णिकामध्ये स्थिरदीपनिभाकृतिं ।
अङ्गुष्ठमात्रमचलं ध्यायेदोंकारमीश्वरम् ।।१९।।

oṃkāraprabhavā devā oṃkāraprabhavāḥ svarāḥ
oṃkāraprabhavaṃ sarvaṃ trailokyaṃ sacarācaram (16)
hrasvo dahati pāpāni dīrghaḥ saṃpatprado 'vyayaḥ
ardhamātrāsamā yuktaḥ praṇavo mokṣadāyaktaḥ (17)
tailadhārāmivācchinnaṃ dīrghaghaṇṭāninādavat
avācyaṃ praṇavasyāgraṃ yastaṃ veda sa vedavit (18)
hṛtpadbhakarṇikāmadhye sthiradīpanibhākṛtiṃ
aṅguṣṭhamātramacalaṃ dhyāyedoṃkāramīśvaram (19)

Anvay

devāḥ: deities; *oṃkāra-prabhavāḥ*: power of *Oṃkāra,* sound of Om; *svarāḥ*: sounds; *sarvam trailokyam*: all the three worlds; *carācaram*: animals [and] plants; *hrasvaḥ*: short; *dahati*: burns; *pāpāni*: sins; *dīrghaḥ*: long one; *avyayaḥ*: imperishable; *saṃpatpradaḥ*: bestows good fortune; *yuktaḥ*: united; *samā*: with; *ardha-mātrā*: half syllable; *praṇavaḥ*: *praṇava*, OM; *dāyaktaḥ*: giver; *mokṣa*: liberation; *iva*: like; *acchinnam*: uninterrupted; *dhārām*: flow; *taila*: oil; *dīrgha ninādavat*: like the long sound; *ghaṇṭā*: bell; *agram*: end; *praṇavasya*: of *praṇava*; *avācyam*: not to be uttered; *yaḥ*: whoever; *veda*: knows; *tam*: this; *vedavit*: knows the true meaning of the Vedas; *dhyāyet*: one should meditate on; *īśvaram*: *Īśvara,* Supreme Reality; *kṛtim*: is like; *sthira-dīpanibhā*: unwavering light; *aṅguṣṭha-mātram*: size of a thumb; *acalam*: motionless; *madhye*: in the centre; *padma-karṇikā*: pericarp of the lotus; *hṛt*: heart.

Translation

Deities [have] the power of *Oṃkāra.* Sounds [have] the power of *Oṃkāra.* All the three worlds [including] animals [and] plants [have] the power of *Oṃkāra.* The short [accent of Om] burns sins; the long one [is] imperishable [and] bestows good fortune. United with the half-syllable, *praṇava* [is] the giver [of] liberation. Like the uninterrupted flow [of] oil [or] like the long sound [of] a bell, the end of *praṇava* [is] not to be uttered. Whoever knows this knows the true meaning of the Vedas. One should meditate on *Oṃkāra* [as] *Īśvara* [who] is like an unwavering light, the size of a thumb [and] motionless in the centre [of] the pericarp of the lotus [of] the heart.

Verses 20 to 25: Oṃkāra Meditation

इडया वायुमापूर्यं पूरयित्वोदरस्थितं ।
ओंकारं देहमध्यस्थं ध्यायेज्ज्वालावलीवृतम् ।।२०।।
ब्रह्मा पूरक इत्युक्तो विष्णुः कुम्भक उच्यते ।
रेचो रुद्र इति प्रोक्तः प्राणायामस्य देवताः ।।२१।।
आत्मानमरणिं कृत्वा प्रणवं चोत्तरारणिम् ।
ध्याननिर्मथनाभ्यासादेव पश्येन्निगूढवत् ।।२२।।
ओंकारध्वनिनादेन वायोः संहरणान्तिकम् ।
यावद्वलं समादध्यात्सम्यङ्नादलयावधि ।।२३।।
गमागमस्थं गमनादिशून्यमोंकारमेकं रविकोटिदीप्तिम् ।
पश्यन्ति ये सर्वजनान्तरस्थं हंसात्मकं ते विरजा भवन्ति
।।२४।।
यन्मनस्त्रिजगात्सृष्टिस्थितिव्यसनकर्मकृत् ।
तन्मनो विलयं याति तद्विष्णोः परम पदम् ।।२५।।

iḍayā vāyumāpūryaṃ pūrayitvodarasthitam
oṃkāraṃ dehamadhyasthaṃ dhyāyejjvālāvalīvṛtam (20)
brahmā pūraka ityukto viṣṇuḥ kumbhaka ucyate
reco rudra iti proktaḥ prāṇāyāmasya devatāḥ (21)
ātmānamaraṇiṃ kṛtvā praṇavaṃ cottarāraṇim
dhyānanirmathanābhyāsādeva paśyennigūḍhavat (22)
oṃkāradhvaninādena vāyoḥ saṃharaṇāntikam
yāvadvalam samādadhyātsamyaṅnādalayāvadhi (23)
gamāgamasthaṃ gamanādiśūnyamoṃkāramekaṃ ravikoṭidīptim
paśyanti ye sarvajanāntarasthaṃ haṃsātmakaṃ te virajā bhavanti (24)
yanmanastrijagātsṛṣṭisthitivyasanakarmakṛt
tanmano vilayaṃ yāti tadviṣṇoḥ parama padam (25)

Anvay

āpūryam: inhaling; *vāyum*: *vāyu*, vital air; *iḍayā*: through the left nostril; *pūrayitva*: filling; *udarasthitam*: whole stomach; *dhyāyet*: one should meditate on; *stham*: being; *deha-madhya*: in the middle [of] the body; *avalī*: concealed; *vṛtam*: surrounded by; *jvāla*: flames; *brahmā*: *Brahmā*, Cosmic Creator; *iti uktaḥ*: is said to be; *pūrakaḥ*: inhalation; *viṣṇuḥ*: Viṣṇu, Preserver of the Universe; *ucyate*: is said to be; *rudraḥ*: Rudra, Transformer; *iti proktaḥ*: is said to be; *recaḥ*: exhalation; *devatāḥ*: deities; *prāṇāyāmasya*: of *prāṇāyāma*, expansion of vital energy; *paśyet*: one can see; *nigūdhavat*: concealed; *abhyāsāt*: through the practice; *dhyāna*: *dhyāna*, contemplation; *kṛtvā*: by making; *ātmānam*: *ātman*, self; *aranim*: *arani*, sacrificial wood; *ca*: and; *praṇavam*: *praṇava*, Aum; *uttara-aranim*: more powerful *arani; ādena*: by hearing; *oṃkāra-dhvanin*: sound [of] *Oṃkāra*; *saṃharaṇa*: restraining; *antikam*: as much as possible; *vāyoḥ*: both inhalation and exhalation; *samādadhyāt*: one should devote oneself to; *valam*: form; *avadhi*: until; *samyak laya*: one is completely absorbed in; *nāda*: inner sound; *ye paśyanti*: those who see; *ekam oṃkāram*: lone *oṃkāra*; *haṃsa-ātmakam*: form of *haṃsa*, sun, Supreme Existence; *sarva-janāntara-stham*: staying in all beings; *dīptim*: shining; *koṭi raviḥ*: ten million suns; *gamāgamastham*: ever going and coming; *śūnya*: devoid of; *gamana*: movement; *te bhavanti*: they become; *virajāḥ*: free from dust; *tat manaḥ*: that intelligence; *yat*: which; *karmakṛt*: originator; *sṛṣṭi*: creation; *sthiti*: preservation; *vyasana*: destruction; *yāti*: becomes; *vilayam*: absorbed; *tat*: that; *parama padam*: Supreme Seat; *viṣṇoḥ*: of Viṣṇu.

Translation

Inhaling *vāyu* through the left nostril, filling the whole stomach, one should meditate on *Oṃkāra* [as] being in the middle [of] the body, concealed [and] surrounded by flames. Brahmā is said to be inhalation; Viṣṇu is said to be breath retention; Rudra is said to be exhalation. [They are] the deities of *prāṇāyāma.* One can see [them], [although] concealed, through the practice of churning, [that is] *dhyāna*, by making the *ātman* the *arani* and *praṇava* the more powerful *arani.* By hearing the sound [of] *Oṃkāra* [and] restraining as much as possible both inhalation and exhalation, one should devote oneself to its form until one is completely absorbed in the inner sound. Those who see the lone *oṃkāra* [as] the form [of] *haṃsa* staying in all beings, shining [like] ten million suns, ever going and coming, devoid of movement, they become free from dust. That intelligence, which [is] the originator [of] creation, preservation [and] destruction in the three worlds, becomes absorbed [in the *Oṃkāra*]. That [is] the Supreme Seat of Viṣṇu.

Verses 26 to 29: Lotus of the Heart

अष्टपत्रं तु हृत्पद्मं द्वात्रंशत्केसरानिवितम् ।
तस्य मध्ये स्थितो भानुर्भानुमध्यगतः शशी ।।२६।।
शशिमध्यगतो वह्निर्वह्निमध्यगता प्रभा ।
प्रभामध्यगतं पीठं नानारत्नप्रवेष्टितम् ।।२७।।
तस्य पीठमध्यगतं वासुदेवं निरञ्जनम् ।
श्रीवत्सकौस्तुभोरस्कं मुक्तामणिविभूषितम् ।।२८।।
शुद्धस्फटिकसंकाशं चन्द्रकोटिसमप्रभम् ।
एवं ध्यायेन्महाविष्णुमेवं वा विनयान्वितः ।।२९।।

aṣṭapatraṃ tu hṛtpadmaṃ dvātraṃśatkesarānivitam
tasya madhye sthito bhānurbhānumadhyagataḥ śaśī (26)
śaśimadhyagato vahnirvahnimadhyagatā prabhā
prabhāmadhyagataṃ pīṭhaṃ nānāratnapraveṣṭitam (27)
tasya pīṭhamadhyagataṃ vāsudevaṃ nirañjanam
śrīvatsakaustubhoraskaṃ muktāmaṇivibhūṣitam (28)
śuddhasphaṭikasaṃkāśaṃ candrakoṭisamaprabham
evaṃ dhyāyenmahāviṣṇumevaṃ vā vinayānvitaḥ (29)

Anvay

itam: now; *hṛt-padmam*: lotus of the heart; *aṣṭa-patram*: eight petals; *dvātraṃśat-kesarāni*: thirty-two staminae; *bhānuḥ*: sun; *tasya madhye*: in its centre; *śaśī*: moon; *gataḥ*: has gone to; *bhānu-madhya*: centre of the sun; *vahniḥ*: *Agni*, deity of fire; *gataḥ*: has gone to; *śaśi-madhya*: centre of the moon; *prabhā*: spiritual light; *vahni-madhya-gatā*: has gone to the centre of *Agni*; *pīṭham*: seat; *praveṣṭitam*: covered with; *nānā-ratna*: many gems; *prabhā-madhya-gatam*: is in the midst of the spiritual light; *nirañjanam vāsudevam*: stainless Vāsudeva, father of Krishna; *madhyagatam*: in the centre; *tasya pīṭha*: of this seat; *śrīvatsa-kaustubhoḥ-askam*: on [his] chest the black mark [and] celebrated jewel; *vibhūṣitam*: adorned with; *muktāmani*: gems and pearls; *saṃkāśam*: resembling; *śuddha sphaṭika*: pure crystal; *samaprabham*: as splendid as; *koṭi*: ten million; *candra*: moons; *evam*: thus; *dhyāyet*: one should meditate on; *vinayānvitaḥ*: humbly; *mahā-viṣṇum*: great Viṣṇu.

Translation

Now the lotus [of] the heart [has] eight petals [and] thirty-two staminae; the sun is in its centre; the moon has gone to the centre of the sun. *Agni* has gone to the centre of the moon; the spiritual light has gone to the centre of *Agni*. The seat, covered with many gems, is in the midst of the spiritual light. [One should hold] the stainless Vāsudeva in the centre [of] this seat, on his chest the black mark [and] celebrated jewel, adorned with gems and pearls, resembling pure crystal [and] as splendid as ten million moons. Thus one should meditate humbly on the great Viṣṇu.

Verses 30 to 35: Meditating on Viṣṇu Brahma and Śiva

अतसीपुष्पसंकाशं नाभिस्थाने प्रतिष्ठितम् ।
चतुर्भुजं महाविष्णुं पूरकेण विचिन्तयेत् ।।३०।।
कुम्भकेन हृदि स्थाने चिन्तयेत्कमलासनम् ।
ब्रह्माणं रक्तगौराभं चतुर्वक्रं पितामहम् ।।३१।।
रेचकेन तु विद्यात्मा ललाटस्थं त्रिलोचनम् ।
शुद्धस्फटिकसंकाशं निष्कलं पापनाशनम् ।।३२।।
अन्नपत्रमधःपुष्पमूर्ध्वनालमधोमुखम् ।
कदलीपुष्पसंकाशं सर्ववेदमयं शिवम् ।।३३।।
शतारं शतपत्राढयं विकीर्णाम्बुजकर्णिकम् ।
तत्रार्कचन्द्रवह्नीनामुपर्यु - परिचिन्तयेत् ।।३४।।
पद्मस्योद्धाटनं कृत्वा बोधचन्द्राग्निसूर्यकम् ।
तस्य हृद्वीजमाहृत्य आत्मानं चरते ध्रुवम् ।।३५।।

atasīpuṣpasaṃkāśaṃ nābhisthāne pratiṣṭhitam
caturbhujaṃ mahāviṣṇuṃ pūrakeṇa vicintayet (30)
kumbhakena hṛdi sthāne cintayetkamalāsanam
brahmāṇaṃ raktagaurābhaṃ caturvakraṃ pitāmaham (31)
recakena tu vidyātmā lalāṭasthaṃ trilocanam
śuddhasphaṭikasaṃkāśaṃ niṣkalaṃ pāpanāśanam (32)
annapatramadhaḥpuṣpamūrdhvanālamadhomukham
kadalīpuṣpasaṃkāśaṃ sarvavedamayaṃ śivam (33)
śatāraṃ śatapatrāḍhayaṃ vikīrṇāmbujakarṇikam
tatrārkacandravahnīnāmuparyu - paricintayet (34)
padmasyoddhāṭanaṃ kṛtvā bodhacandrāgnisūryakam
tasya hṛdvījamāhṛtya ātmānaṃ carate dhruvam (35)

Anvay

pūrakeṇa: on inhalation; *vicintayet*: one should meditate on;

caturbhujam mahāviṣṇum: four-armed Mahā Viṣṇu; *saṃkāśam*: resembling; *atasī-puṣpa*: *atasī* (flax) flower; *pratiṣṭhitam*: situated; *sthāne*: in the area; *nābhi*: navel; *kumbhakena*: on retention of breath; *cintayet*: one should meditate on; *sthāne*: in the area; *hṛdi*: of the heart; *pitāmaham brahmānam*: Grandfather Brahman; *caturvakram*: with four faces; *raktagauḥ-ābham*: reddish-yellow lustre; *kamala-āsanam*: seated on a lotus; *tu*: then; *recakena*: on exhalation; *vidyā-ātmā*: knowledge of the Self; *lalātstham*: eyebrow centre; *trilocanam*: three-eyed Śiva; *niṣkalam*: stainless; *pāpanāśanam*: destroying all sins; *saṃkāśam*: resembling; *śuddha-sphaṭika*: pure crystal; *śivam*: Śiva; *mayam*: form; *sarva-veda*: all the vedas; *saṃkāśam*: like; *puṣpam*: flower; *kadalī*: plantain tree; *mukham*: face; *adhaḥ*: down; *nālam*: stalk; *ūrdhva*: above; *anna*: nourishing; *patram*: leaf; *puṣpam*: flower; *adhaḥ*: below; *karṇikam*: pericarp; *ambuja*: lotus; *vikīrṇa*: filled with; *śatāram*: at a hundred angles; *śata-patra-āḍhayam*: hundred petals and others; *tatra*: there; *paricintayet*: one should meditate on; *ārka-candra-vahnīnām*: sun, moon [and] Vahni, deviate of Agni; *uparyu*: up high; *uddha-aṭanam kṛtvā*: having moved up; *padmasya*: through the lotus; *bodha*: consciousness; *sūryakam*: resembles the Sun; *agni*: power of fire; *candra*: Moon; *vījam āhṛtya*: moistening; *hṛd*: heart; *tasya*: with it; *dhruvam*: definitely; *carate*: reaches; *ātmānam*: Self.

Translation

On inhalation one should meditate on the four-armed Mahā Viṣṇu resembling the *atasī* flower [and] situated in the area [of] the navel. On retention of breath, one should meditate in the area of the heart on the Grandfather Brahman with four faces [and] a reddish-yellow lustre, seated [on] a lotus. Then, on exhalation, for knowledge of the Self [one should meditate] at the eyebrow centre on the three-eyed Śiva, stainless, destroying all sins, resembling pure crystal; Śiva, the form of all the Vedas, like the flower of the plantain tree, its face down, stalk above, nourishing the leaf [and] the flower below, the pericarp [of the] lotus filled at a hundred angles with a hundred petals and others. There one should meditate upon the sun, the moon and Vahni up high. Having moved up through the lotus [whose] consciousness resembles the Sun, Agni [and] the Moon, [and] moistening [his] heart with it, he definitely reaches the Self.

Verses 36 and 37: Knowledge of the Vedas

त्रिस्थानं च त्रिमात्रं च त्रिब्रह्म च त्रयाक्षरम् ।
त्रिमात्रमर्धमात्रं वा यस्तं वेद स वेदवित् ।।३६।।
तैलधारामिवाच्छिन्नदीर्घघण्टानिनादवत् ।
बिन्दुनादकलातीतं यस्तं वेद स वेदवित् ।।३७।।

tristhānaṃ ca trimātraṃ ca tribrahma ca trayākṣaram
trimātramardhamātraṃ vā yastaṃ veda sa vedavit (36)
tailadhārāmivācchinnadīrghaghaṇṭāninādavat
bindunādakalātītaṃ yastaṃ veda sa vedavit (37)

Anvay

yaḥ: whoever; *vedavit*: knows; *tristhānam*: three seats; *trimātram*: three *mātras*; *tribrahmaḥ*: three Brahmas; *ca*: and; *trayākṣaram*: three akṣaras; *vā*: or; *trimātram*: three *mātras*; *ardha-mātram*: half *mātra*; *sa*: he; *tam vedaḥ*: the knowledge of the Vedas; *yaḥ*: whoever; *vedavit*: knows; *atītam*: has surpassed; *bindu*: Supreme Point; *nāda*: Inner Sound; *kalā*: elements; *acchinna*: uninterrupted; *iva*: like; *dhārām*: stream; *taila*: oil; *dīrgha ninādavat*: as long as the sound; *ghaṇṭā*: bell; *sa*: he; *tam vedaḥ*: the knowledge of the Vedas.

Translation

Whoever knows the three seats, the three mātras, the three Brahmas and the three akṣaras, or the three mātras [of] the half-mātra, he [has] the knowledge of the Vedas. Whoever knows [that that which] has surpassed *bindu*, nāda [and] *kalā* [is] uninterrupted like a stream [of] oil [and] as long as the sound [of] a bell, he [has] the knowledge of the Vedas.

Verses 38 to 40: Abode of the Supreme Spirit

यथैवोत्पलनालेन तोयमाकर्षयेन्नरः ।
तथैवोत्कर्षयेद्वायुं योगी योगपथे स्थितः ।।३८।।
अर्धमात्रात्पकं कृत्वा कोशीभूतं तु पङ्कजम् ।
कर्षयेन्नालमात्रेण भ्रुवोर्मध्ये लयं नयेत् ।।३९।।
भ्रुवोर्मध्ये ललाटे तु नासिकायास्तु मूलतः ।
जानीयादमृतं स्थानं तद्ब्रह्मायतनं महत् ।।४०।।

yathaivotpalanālena toyamākarṣayennaraḥ
tathaivotkarṣayedvāyuṃ yogī yogapathe sthitaḥ (38)
ardhamātrātpakaṃ kṛtvā kośībhūtaṃ tu paṅkajam
karṣayennālamātreṇa bhruvormadhye layaṃ nayet (39)
bhruvormadhye lalāte tu nāsikāyāstu mūlataḥ
jānīyādamṛtaṃ sthānaṃ tadbrahmāyatanaṃ mahat (40)

Anvay

yatha eva: just as; *naraḥ*: man; *ākarṣayet*: draws up; *toyam*: water; *nālena*: through the hollow stalk; *utpala*: lotus; *tatha eva*: so; *yogī*: yogin; *sthitaḥ*: established; *yoga-pathe*: on the path of yoga; *utkarṣayet*: should draw in; *vāyum*: breath; *kṛtvā*: having made; *kośībhūtam*: seed vessel; *paṅkajam*: lotus flower; *ardhamātrātpakam*: in the form of *ardhamātrā*; *karṣayet*: he should draw; *nālamātreṇa*: through the stalk of the *mātrā*; *layam nayet*: he should absorb; *bhruvormadhye*: at the eyebrow centre; *jānīyāt*: he should know; *sthānam*: seat; *amṛtam*: nectar; *mūlataḥ*: base; *nāsikāyāḥ*: of the nose; *tu . . . tu*: as well as; *bhruvormadhye*: at the eyebrow centre; *lalāte*: in the forehead; *tad*: this; *mahat āyatanam*: great abode; *brahma*: Supreme Spirit.

Translation

Just as a man draws up water through the hollow stalk [of] a lotus, so should the yogin, established on the path of yoga, draw in the breath. Having made the seed vessel [of] the lotus flower in the form of *ardhamātrā*, he should draw [the breath] through the stalk of the *mātrā*, [and] absorb [it] at the eyebrow centre. He should know [that] the seat [of] nectar [is] the base of the nose as well as at the eyebrow centre in the forehead. This [is] the great abode [of] the Supreme Spirit.

Verse 41: Six Limbs of Yoga

आसनानि प्राणसंरोधः प्रत्याहारश्च धारणा ।
ध्यानं समाधिरेतानि योगाङ्गानि भवन्ति षट् ।।४१।।

āsanāni prāṇasaṃrodhaḥ pratyāhāraśca dhāraṇā
dhyānaṃ samādhiretāni yogāṅgāni bhavanti ṣaṭ (41)

Anvay

āsanāni: postures; *prāṇa-saṃrodhaḥ*: restraint of breath; *pratyāhāraḥ*: withdrawal of the senses; *dhāraṇā*: concentration; *dhyānam*: meditation; *ca*: and; *samādhiḥ*: self-realisation; *etāni*: these; *bhavanti*: are; *ṣaṭ yoga-aṅgāni*: six limbs of yoga.

Translation

Postures, restraint of breath, withdrawal of the senses; concentration, meditation and self-realisation: these are the six limbs of yoga.

Verses 42 and 43a: Main Postures

आसनानि च तावन्ति यावन्त्यो जीवजातयः ।

एतेषामतुलान्भेदा न्विजानाति महेश्वरः ।।४२।।

सिद्धं भद्रं तथा सिम्हं पद्मं चेति चतुष्टयम् ।४३।

āsanāni ca tāvanti yāvantyo jīvajātayaḥ
eteṣāmatulānbhedānvijānāti maheśvaraḥ (42)
siddhaṃ bhadraṃ tathā simhaṃ padmaṃ ceti catuṣṭayam (43a)

Anvay

yāvantyaḥ tāvanti: as many as; *jīvajātayaḥ*: living creatures; *āsanāni*: postures; *ca*: and; *maheśvaraḥ*: Great Lord; *vijānāti*: recognises; *eteṣām-atulān-bhedān*: their incomparable differences; *iti*: it is said; *siddham*: *siddha*, perfected pose; *bhadram*: *bhadra,* gracious pose; *tathā*: as well as; *simham*: *simha*, lion pose; *ca*: and; *padmam*: *padma*, lotus pose; *catuṣṭayam*: four.

Translation

[There are] as many living creatures as [there are] postures, and the Great Lord recognises their incomparable differences. It is said [that] *siddha, bhadra,* as well as *simha* and *padma* [are] the four [main postures].

Verses 43b to 50a: First Three Cakras

आधारं प्रथमं चक्रं स्वाधिष्ठानं द्वितीयकम् ।।४३।।
योनिस्थानं तयोर्मध्ये कामरूप निगद्यते ।
आधाराख्ये गुदस्थाने पङ्कजं यच्चतुर्दलम् ।।४४।।
तन्मध्ये प्रोच्यते योनिः कामाख्या सिद्धवन्दिता ।
योनिमध्ये स्थितं लिङ्गं पश्चिमाभिमुखं तथा ।।४५।।
मस्तके मणिवभ्दिन्नं यो जानाति स योगवित्
तप्तचामीकराकारं तडिल्लेखेव विस्फुरत् ।।४६।।
चतुरस्रमुपर्यग्नेरधो मेढ्रात्प्रतिष्ठितम्
स्वशब्देन भवेत्प्राणः स्वाधिष्ठानं तदाश्रयम् ।।४७।।
स्वादिष्ठानं ततश्चक्रं मेढ्रमेव निगद्यते
मणिवत्तन्तुना यत्र वायुना पूरितं वपुः ।।४८।।
तन्नाभिमण्डलं चक्रं प्रोच्यते मणिपूरकं ।
द्वादशारमहाचक्रे पुण्यपापनियन्त्रितः ।।४९।।
तावज्जीवो भ्रमत्येवं यावत्तत्त्वं न विन्दति ।५०।

ādhāraṃ prathamaṃ cakraṃ svādhisthānaṃ dvitīyakam (43b)
yonisthānaṃ tayormadhye kāmarūpa nigadyate
ādhārākhye gudasthāne paṅkajaṃ yaccaturdalam (44)
tanmadhye procyate yoniḥ kāmākhyā siddhavanditā
yonimadhye sthitaṃ liṅgaṃ paścimābhimukhaṃ tathā (45)
mastake maṇivabhdinnaṃ yo jānāti sa yogavit
taptacāmīkarākāraṃ taḍillekheva visphurat (46b)
caturasramuparyagneradho meḍhrātpratiṣṭhitam
svaśabdena bhavetprāṇaḥ svādhiṣṭhānaṃ tadāśrayam (47b)
svādhiṣṭhānam tataścakraṃ meḍhrameva nigadyate
maṇivattantunā yatra vāyunā pūritaṃ vapuḥ (48b)
tannābhimaṅḍalaṃ cakraṃ procyate maṇipūrakam
dvādaśāramahācakre puṇyapāpaniyantritaḥ (49)

tāvajjīvo bhramatyevaṃ yāvattattvaṃ na vindati (50a)

Anvay

prathamam cakram: first cakra; *ādhāram*: base; *dvitīyakam*: second; *svādhiṣṭhānam*: *svādhiṣṭhāna*; *tayoḥ-madhye*: between these two; *nigadyate*: is said; *yoni-sthānam*: site of *yoni*, perineum; *kāma-rūpa*: form of *Kāma*; *caturdalam*: four-petalled; *paṅkajam*: lotus; *guda-sthāne*: in the site of the anus; *ādhāra-ākhye*: called the base; *tat-madhye*: in the middle of it; *procyate*: is said; *kāma-ākhyā*: called *Kāma*; *siddha-vanditā*: extolled by the *siddhas*; *yoni-madhye*: in the centre of the yoni; *sthitam*: stands; *liṅgam*: *liṅgam*; *abhimukham*: facing; *paścima*: west; *abhdinnam*: split; *mastake*: at the top; *iva maṇi*: like a precious stone; *yaḥ*: whoever; *jānāti*: knows; *yogavit*: knower of yoga; *caturasram*: quadrangular figure; *ākāram*: form; *tapta-cāmīkarākāra*: molten gold; *visphurat*: flashing; *iva*: like; *tadillekhāḥ*: streaks of lightning; *pratiṣṭhitam*: situated; *upari agni*: above *agni*; *adhaḥ*: below; *medhrāt*: genital organ; *prāṇam*: prāṇa; *Tat*: whose; *āśrayam*: seat; *svādhiṣṭhānam*: Svādhiṣṭhāna; *bhavet*: arises; *sva-śabdena*: with its own sound; *tataḥ*: thus; *cakram svādhiṣṭhānam*: cakra Svādhiṣṭhāna; *eva*: even; *nigadyate*: is referred to as; *meḍhram*: genital organ; *tat cakram*: that cakra; *nābhi-maṇḍalam*: within the orb of the navel; *yatra*: where; *vapuḥ*: body; *pūritam*: filled; *vāyunā*: with air; *maṇivat*: like jewels; *tantunā*: with a string; *procyate*: is called; *maṇipūrakam*: *Maṇipūra,* city of jewels; *jīvaḥ*: *jīva*; *niyantritaḥ*: governed by; *puṇya-pāpa*: pure [and] sinful; *bhramati*: spins about; *mahā-cakre*: in [this] great cakra; *dvādaśāra*: twelve spokes; *yāvat . . tāvat*: as long . . as; *na vindati*: it does not experience; *tattvam*: true state.

Translation

[The site of] the first cakra [is] the base [and] the second [is] *svādhiṣṭhāna.* Between these two is said [to be] the site of *yoni* in the form of *Kāma.* [There is] a four-petalled lotus in the site of the anus, called the base [cakra]. In the middle of it is said [to be] the yoni called Kāma, extolled by the *siddhas.* In the centre of the yoni stands the *liṅgam*, facing west [and] split at the top like a precious stone. Whoever knows [this is] a knower of yoga. A quadrangular figure, [in] the form [of] molten gold [and] flashing like streaks of lightning, [is] situated above agni [and] below the genital organ. Prāṇa, whose seat is Svādhiṣṭhāna, arises with its own sound. Thus the cakra Svādhiṣṭhāna is even referred to as the genital organ. That cakra [within] the orb of the navel, where the body [is] filled with air like jewels with a string, is called *Maṇipūra*, city of jewels. The *jīva*, governed by [its] pure [and] sinful [actions], spins about in [this] great cakra [of] twelve spokes as long as it does not experience [its] true state.

Verses 50b to 53: Nāḍīs

ऊर्ध्वं मेढ्रादधो नाभेः कन्दो यो ऽस्ति खगाण्डवत् ।।५०।।
तत्र नाड्यः समुत्पन्नाः सहस्राणि द्विसप्ततिः ।
तेषु नाडीसहस्रेषु द्विसप्ततिरुदाहृताः ।।५१।।
प्रधानाः प्राणवाहिन्यो भूयस्तत्र दश स्मृताः ।
इडा च पिङ्गला चैव सुषुम्ना च तृतीयका ।।५२।।
गाम्धारी हस्तिजिह्वा च पूषा चैव यशस्विनी ।
अलम्बुसा कुहूरत्र शङ्खिनी दशमी स्मृता ।।५३।।

ūrdhvaṃ medhrādadho nābheḥ kando yo 'sti khagāṅḍavat (50b)
tatra nādyaḥ samutpannāḥ sahasrāṇi dvisaptatiḥ
teṣu nāḍīsahasreṣu dvisaptatirudāhṛtāḥ (51)
pradhānāḥ prāṇavāhinyo bhūyastatra daśa smṛtāḥ
iḍā ca piṅgalā caiva suṣumnā ca tṛtīyakā (52)
gāmdhārī hastijihvā ca pūṣā caiva yaśasvinī
alambusā kuhūratra śaṅkhinī daśamī smṛtā (53)

Anvay

ūrdhvam medhrāt: above the genital organ; *adhaḥ nābheḥ*: below the navel; *asti*: is; *kandaḥ*: knot; *khaga-āṅḍavat*: like a bird's egg; *tatra*: from there; *samutpannāḥ*: arise; *dvisaptatiḥ sahasrāṇi*: seventy-two thousand; *nādyaḥ*: nāḍīs; *teṣu nāḍī-sahasreṣu*: of these thousands of nāḍīs; *dvisaptatiḥ*: seventy-two; *udāhṛtāḥ*: are recognised; *tatra*: of these; *smṛtāḥ*: it is declared; *daśa*: ten; *pradhānāḥ*: main ones; *prāṇa-vāhinyaḥ*: carry the prāṇas; *daśamī*: ten; *smṛtā*: are said to be; *tṛtīyakā*: triplicate; *iḍā*: ida, left nāḍī; *piṅgalā*: piṅgalā, right nāḍī; *ca*: and; *suṣumnā*: suṣumnā, central nāḍī; *ca eva*: as well as.

Translation

Above the genital organ [and] below the navel is a knot like a bird's egg. From there arise seventy-two thousand nāḍīs. Of these thousands of nāḍīs, seventy-two are recognised. Of these it is declared [there are] ten main ones [which] carry the prāṇas. The ten are said to be the triplicate iḍā, piṅgalā and suṣumnā, and gāndhārī, hastijihvā and pūṣā as well as yaśasvinī, alambusā, kuhūratra [and] śaṅkhinī.

Verses 54 to 58a: Nāḍīs and Prāṇa

एवं नाडीमयं चक्रं विज्ञेयं योगिना सदा ।

सततं प्राणवाहिन्यः सोमसूर्याग्निदेवताः ।।५४।।

इडापिङ्गलासुषुम्नास्तिस्रो नाड्यः प्रकीर्तिताः ।

इडा वामे स्थिता भागे पिङ्गला दक्षिणे स्थिता ।।५५।।

सुषुम्ना मध्यदेशे तु प्राणमार्गास्त्रयः स्मृताः ।

प्राणो ऽपानः समानश्चोदानो व्यानस्तथैव च ।।५६।।

नागः कूर्मः कृकरको देवदत्तो धनंजयः ।

प्राणादाः पञ्च विख्याता नागाद्याः पञ्च वायवः ।।५७।।

एते नाडीसहस्रेषु वर्तन्ते जीवरूपिणः ।५८।

evaṃ nāḍīmayaṃ cakraṃ vijñeyaṃ yoginā sadā
satataṃ prāṇavāhinyaḥ somasūryāgnidevatāḥ (54)
iḍāpiṅgalāsuṣumnāstisro nāḍyaḥ prakīrtitāḥ
iḍā vāme sthitā bhāge piṅgalā dakṣine sthitā (55)
suṣumnā madhyadeśe tu prāṇamārgāsrayaḥ smṛtāḥ
prāṇo 'pānaḥ samānaścodāno vyānastathaiva ca (56)
nāgaḥ kūrmaḥ kṛkarako devadatto dhanaṃjayaḥ
prāṇādāḥ pañca vikhyātā nāgādyāḥ pañca vāyavaḥ (57)
ete nāḍīsahasreṣu vartante jīvarūpiṇaḥ (58a)

Anvay

evam: thus; *cakram*: cakra; *nāḍī-mayam*: containing the nāḍīs; *sadā*: always; *vijñeyam*: should be understood; *yoginā*: by the yogin; *tisraḥ nāḍyaḥ*: three nāḍīs; *iḍā*: ida, left nadi; *piṅgalā*: piṅgalā, right nāḍī; *suṣumnā*: suṣumnā, central nāḍī; *devatāḥ*: deities; *soma*: Moon; *sūrya*: Sun; *agni*: Agni, deity of fire; *prakīrtitāḥ*: are said to; *prāṇa-vāhinyaḥ*: carry the prāṇas; *satatam*: continuously; *sthitā*: is; *vāme bhāge*: on the left side; *dakṣine*: on the right; *tu*: and; *madhyadeśe*: in the middle; *smṛtāḥ*: they are known to be; *prāṇa-mārgāḥ-rayaḥ*: flowing paths of prāṇa; *prāṇah*: *prāṇa*; *upānah*: *Upāna*; *samāna*: *Samāna*; *udānaḥ*: *Udāna*; *ca tatha*: and then; *nāgaḥ*: *Nāga*; *kūrmaḥ*: *Kūrma*; *kṛkarakaḥ*: *Kṛkaraka*; *devadattaḥ*: *Devadatta*; *ca*: and; *dhanaṃjayaḥ*: *Dhanaṃjaya*; *ādyāḥ pañca*: first five; *vikhyātāḥ*: are called; *pañca nāga-ādyāḥ*: five beginning with Nāga; *vāyavaḥ*: *vāyavas*, coming from the air; *ete*: these; *jīva-rūpiṇaḥ*: forms of life; *vartante*: move along; *nāḍī-sahasreṣu*: thousands of nāḍīs.

Translation

Thus the cakra containing the nāḍīs should always be understood by the yogin. The three nāḍīs, iḍā, piṅgalā [and] suṣumnā, [whose] deities [are] the Moon, Sun [and] Agni, are said to carry the prāṇas continuously. Iḍā is on the left side, piṅgalā on the right and suṣumnā in the middle. They are known to be the flowing paths of prāṇa. *Prāṇa, Upāna, Samāna, Udāna* and then *Nāga, Kūrma, Kṛkaraka, Devadatta* and *Dhanaṃjaya*: the first five are called prāṇas, [and] the five beginning with Nāga [are called] *vāyavas*. These forms of life move along the thousands of nāḍīs.

Verses 58b to 61a: Jīva

प्राणापानवशो जीवो ह्यधश्चोर्ध्वं प्रधावति ।।५८।।
वामदक्षिणमार्गेण चन्चलत्वान्न दृश्यते ।
आक्षिप्तो भुजदण्देन यथोच्चलति कन्दुका ।।५९।।
प्राणापानसमाक्षिप्तस्तद्वज्जीवो न विश्रमेत् ।
अपानात्कर्षति प्राणो ऽपानः प्राणाच्च कर्षति ।।६०।।
खगरज्जुवदित्येतद्यो जानाति स योगवित् ।६१।

prāṇāpānavaśo jīvo hyadhaścordhvaṃ pradhāvati (58b)
vāmadakṣiṇamārgeṇa cancalatvānna dṛśyate
ākṣipto bhujadaṇdena yathoccalati kandukā (59)
prāṇāpānasamākṣiptastadvajjīvo na viśramet
apānātkarṣati prāṇo 'pānaḥ prāṇācca karṣati (60)
khagarajjuvadityetadyo jānāti sa yogavit (61a)

Anvay

jīvaḥ: jīva, life; *vaśaḥ*: dependent on; *prāṇa-apāna*: prāṇa and apāna, upward and downward energy; *pradhāvati*: spreads; *adhaḥ*: downwards; *ūrdhvam*: upwards; *cancalatvāt*: because it fluctuates; *vāma-dakṣiṇa-mārgeṇa*: between the left and right paths; *na dṛśyate*: one cannot see; *yatha*: just as; *kandukaḥ*: ball; *ut-calati*: bounces up; *ākṣiptaḥ*: thrown down; *bhuja-daṇdena*: with the stick in one's hand; *tadvat*: so; *samākṣiptaḥ*: hurled about; *prāṇa-apāna*: prāṇa and apana; *na viśramet*: cannot rest; *karṣati*: draws; *apānāt*: from apāna; *ca*: and; *prāṇaat*: from prāṇa; *iti*: it is said; *khaga-rajju-vat*: like a bird from a rope; *yaḥ jānāti*: whoever knows; *etat*: this; *yogavit*: is a knower of yoga.

Translation

Jīva, [being] dependent on prāṇa and apāna, spreads downwards [and] upwards. Because it fluctuates between the left and right paths, one cannot see [it]. Just as a ball bounces up, [after] being thrown down with the stick in one's hand, so the jīva, hurled about [by] prāṇa and apāna, cannot rest. Prāṇa draws [itself] from apāna, and apāna draws [itself] from prāṇa, it is said like a bird from a rope. Whoever knows this is a knower of yoga.

Verses 61b to 65a: Mantra Haṃsa Haṃsa

हकारेण बहिर्याति सकारेण विशेत्पुनः ॥६१॥
हंसहंसेत्यमुं मन्त्रं जीवो जपति सर्वदा ।
शतानि षट्दिवारात्रं सहस्राण्येकविंशतिः ॥६२॥
एतत्संख्यान्वितं मन्त्रं जीवो जपति सर्वदा ।
अजपा नाम गायत्री योगिनां मोक्षदा सदा ॥६३॥
अस्याः संकल्पमात्रेण नरः पापैः प्रमुच्यते ।
अनया सदृशी विद्या अनया सदृशो जपः ॥६४॥
अनया सदृशं पुण्यं न भूतं न भविष्यति ।६५।

hakāreṇa bahiryāti sakāreṇa viśetpunaḥ (61b)
haṃsahaṃsetyamuṃ mantraṃ jīvo japati sarvadā
śatāni ṣaṭūdivārātraṃ sahasrāṇyekaviṃśatiḥ (62)
etatsaṃkhyānvitaṃ mantraṃ jīvo japati sarvadā
ajapā nāma gāyatrī yogināṃ mokṣadā sadā (63)
asyāḥ saṃkalpamātreṇa naraḥ pāpaiḥ pramucyate
anayā sadṛśī vidyā anayā sadṛśo japaḥ (64)
anayā sadṛśaṃ puṇyaṃ na bhūtaṃ na bhaviṣyati (65a)

Anvay

jīvaḥ: jīva; *bahir-yāti*: goes out; *hakāreṇa*: with the sound Ha; *viśet*: enters; *punaḥ*: again; *sakāreṇa*: with the sound Sa; *iti*: thus; *sarvadā*: always; *japati*: repeating; *amum mantram haṃsa-haṃsa*: that mantra *haṃsa haṃsa; jīvaḥ japati sarvadā*: jīva always repeats; *etat mantram*: this mantra; *sahasrāṇi-eka-viṃśatiḥ*: twenty-one thousand; *ṣaṭū śatāni*: six hundred; *saṃkhyānvitam*: times; *divā-rātram*: day and night; *nāma*: by name; *sadā*: forever; *mokṣa-dā*: giving liberation; *yoginām*: to the yogin; *naraḥ*: man; *pramucyate*: is freed; *pāpaiḥ*: from sins; *saṃkalpa-mātreṇa*: simply by the thought; *asyāḥ*: of it; *na bhūtam*: neither in the past; *na bhaviṣyati*: nor in the future; *vidyā*: science; *sadṛśī*: equal; *anayā*: to this; *japaḥ*: *japa*; *sadṛśaḥ anayā*: equivalent to this; *puṇyam*: virtuous act; *sadṛśam*: level; *anayā*: with this.

Translation

Jīva goes out with the sound Ha, [and] enters again with the sound Sa, thus always repeating that mantra *Haṃsa Haṃsa.* Jīva always repeats this mantra twenty-one thousand six hundred times day and night, *ajapā gāyatrī* by name, forever giving liberation to the yogin. A man is freed from sins simply by the thought of it. Neither in the past nor in the future [is there] a science equal to this, a *japa* equivalent to this [or] a virtuous act level with this.

Verses 65b to 68: Parameśvarī

येन मार्गेण गन्तव्यं ब्रह्मस्थानं निरामयम् ।।६५।।
मुखेनाच्छाद्य तद्द्वारं प्रसुप्ता परमेश्वरी ।
प्रबुद्धा वह्नियोगेन मनसा मरुता सह ।।६६।।
सूचिवद्गुणमादाय व्रजत्यूर्ध्वं सुषुम्नया ।
उद्घाटयेत्कपाटं तु यथा कुञ्चिकया हठात् ।।६७।।
कुण्डलिन्या तया योगी मोक्षद्वारं विभेदयेत् ।।६८।।

yena mārgeṇa gantavyaṃ brahmasthānaṃ nirāmayam (65b)
mukhenācchādya taddvāraṃ prasuptā parameśvarī
prabuddhā vahniyogena manasā marutā saha (66)
sūcivadguṇamādāya vrajatyūrdhvaṃ suṣumnayā
udghāṭayetkapāṭaṃ tu yathā kuñcikayā haṭhāt (67)
kuṇḍalinyā tayā yogī mokṣadvāraṃ vibhedayet (68)

Anvay

parameśvarī: *Parameśvarī, kuṇḍalini śakti*; *prasuptā*: sleeps; *ācchādya*: having covered; *mukhena*: with her mouth; *tat dvāram*: that door; *yena mārgeṇa*: through which way; *gantavyam*: leads to; *nirāmayam*: untainted; *brahma-sthānam*: place of Brahma; *prabuddhā*: awakened; *vahni-yogena*: by the union of agni; *saha manasā marutā*: with manas [and] prāṇa; *ādāya*: having taken; *sūcivat*: needle-like; *guṇam*: quality; *vrajati ūrdhvam*: she passes upwards; *suṣumnayā*: through suṣumnā; *yathā*: just as; *kuñcikayā*: with a key; *yogī*: yogin; *udghāṭayet*: should open; *kapātam*: door; *haṭhāt*: with full force; *vibhedayet*: should split; *mokṣa-dvāram*: door to liberation; *tayā kuṇḍalinyā*: by means of the kuṇḍalinī.

Translation

Parameśvarī sleeps, having covered with her mouth that door through which way leads to the untainted place of Brahma.

[Then] awakened by the union of agni with manas [and] prāṇa, having taken a needle-like quality, she passes upwards through suṣumnā. Just as with a key, the yogin should open [this] door with full force [and] split the door to liberation by means of the kuṇḍalinī.

Verse 69: Raising Prāṇa

कृत्वा संपुटितौ करौ दृढतरं बद्ध्वाथ पद्मासनं गाढं वक्षसि

सन्निधाय चुबुकं ध्यानं च तच्चेतसि ।

वारंवारमपातमूर्ध्वमनिलं प्रोच्चारयन्पूरितं मुञ्चन्प्राणमुपैति

बोधमतुलं शक्तिप्रभावान्नरः ॥६९॥

kṛtvā saṃpuṭitau karau dṛḍhataraṃ baddhātha padmāsanaṃ gāḍhaṃ vakṣasi sannidhāya cubukaṃ dhyānaṃ ca taccetasi vāraṃvāramapātamūrdhvamanilaṃ proccārayanpūritaṃ muñcanprāṇamupaiti bodhamatulaṃ śaktiprabhāvānnaraḥ (69)

Anvay

kṛtvā saṃpuṭitau: folding; *karau*: hands; *dṛḍhataram*: firmly; *atha*: then; *baddhā*: fixed in; *padmāsanam*: *padmāsana*; *sannidhāya*: placing; *cubukam*: chin; *gāḍham*: firmly; *vakṣasi*: on the chest; *ca*: and; *dhyānam*: *dhyāna*; *cetasi*: on the mind; *vāraṃvāram*: repeatedly; *apātam*: raise; *anilam*: vital air; *ūrdhvam*: upwards; *pūritam*: inhale; *proccārayan*: forcefully; *upaiti*: and then; *muñcat*: release; *prāṇam*: prāṇa; *naraḥ*: man; *atulam*: unequalled; *bodham*: wisdom; *prabhāvāt śakti*: through [this] splendid *śakti.*

Translation

Folding the hands firmly, then fixed in *padmāsana,* placing the chin firmly on the chest and *dhyāna* on the mind, [one should] repeatedly raise the vital air upwards, inhale forcefully, and then release the prāṇa. A man [obtains] unequalled wisdom through [this] splendid *śakti*.

Verse 70: Doors of the Nāḍīs

पद्मासनस्थितो योगी नाडीद्वारेषु पूरयन् ।
मारुतं कुम्भयन्यस्तु स मुक्तो नात्र संशयः ॥७०॥

padmāsanasthito yogī nāḍīdvāreṣu pūrayan
mārutaṃ kumbhayanyastu sa mukto nātra saṃśayaḥ (70)

Anvay

yogī yaḥ: yogin who; *padmāsana-sthitaḥ*: seated in padmāsana; *pūrayan*: inhales; *kumbhayan*: restrains; *mārutam*: breath; *nāḍī-dvāreṣu*: at the doors of the nāḍīs; *na saṃśayaḥ*: without doubt; *muktaḥ*: liberated; *atra*: here.

Translation

The yogin who, seated in padmāsana, inhales [and] restrains the breath at the doors of the nāḍīs, is without doubt liberated here.

Verses 71 to 73: Awakening kuṇḍalinī

अङ्गानां मर्दनं कृत्वा श्रमजातेन वारिणा ।
कट्वम्ललवणत्यागी क्षीरपानरतः सुखी ।।७१।।
ब्रह्मचारी मिताहारी योगी योगपरायणः ।
अब्दादूर्ध्वं भवेत्सिद्धो नात्र कार्या विचारणा ।।७२।।
कन्दोर्ध्वकुण्डली शक्तिः स योगी सिद्धिभाजनम् ।
अपानप्राणयोरैक्यं क्षयान्मूत्रपुरीषयोः ।।७३।।

aṅgānāṃ mardanaṃ kṛtvā śramajātena vāriṇā
kaṭvamlalavaṇatyāgī kṣīrapānarataḥ sukhī (71)
brahmacārī mitāhārī yogī yogaparāyanaḥ
abdādūrdhvaṃ bhavetsiddho nātra kāryā vicāraṇā (72)
kandordhvakuṇḍalī śaktiḥ sa yogī siddhibhājanam
apānaprāṇayoraikyaṃ kṣayānmūtrapurīṣayoḥ (73)

Anvay

kṛtvā mardanam: having wiped; *aṅgānām*: from the limbs; *vāriṇā*: sweat; *śrama-jātena*: produced by fatigue; *yāgī*: forgoing; *kaṭvam*: pungent; *lalavanat*: causes one to salivate; *yogī*: yogin; *yoga-parāyanaḥ*: wholly devoted to yoga; *S sukhī pānarataḥ*: loves to drink; *kṣīra*: milk; *brahmacārī*: celibate; *mitāhārī*: eats moderately; *bhavet-siddhaḥ*: becomes a *siddha*; *ūrdhvam abdāt*: in just over a year; *na vicāraṇā*: no investigation; *kāryā*: needs to be done; *atra*: in this respect; *kuṇḍalī śaktiḥ*: kuṇḍalinī śakti; *ūrdhva kanda*: up in the throat; *apāna-prāṇayoḥ-aikyam*: apāna [and] prāṇa are united; *kṣayāt*: ending; *mūtra-purīṣayoḥ*: urine [and] faeces; *yogī*: yogin; *siddhi-bhājanam*: receives siddhis.

Translation

Having wiped from the limbs the sweat produced by fatigue, forgoing [food which is] pungent [and] causes one to salivate, the yogin [who is] wholly devoted to yoga, loves to drink milk, [is] celibate [and] eats moderately, becomes a *siddha* in just over a year. No investigation needs to be done in this respect. [When] kuṇḍalinī śakti [is] up in the throat, [then] apāna [and] prāṇa are united, ending [the production of] urine [and] faeces, [and] the yogin receives siddhis.

Verses 74 and 75a: Mūlabandha

युवा भवति वृध्दोऽपि सततं मूलबन्धनात् ।
पार्ष्णिभागेन संपीद्य योनिमाकुञ्चयेद्गुदम् ।।७४।।
अपानमूर्ध्वमुत्कृश्य मूलबन्धोऽयमुच्यते ।७५।

yuvā bhavati vṛdhdo 'pi satataṃ mūlabandhanāt
pārṣṇibhāgena saṃpīdya yonimākuñcayedgudam (74)
apānamūrdhvamutkṛśya mūlabandho 'yamucyate. (75a)

Anvay
api: even; *vṛdhdaḥ*: old person; *bhavati*: becomes; *yuvā*: young; *satataṃ mūlabandhanāt*: through constant mūlādhāra; *saṃpīdya*: pressing; *yonim*: yoni; *bhāgena*: with part; *pārṣṇi*: heel; *ākuñcayet*: one should contract; *gudam*: anus; *utkṛśya*: while raising; *apānam*: apāna; *ūrdhvam*: upwards; *ayam ucyate*: this is called; *mūlabandhaḥ*: mūlabandha.

Translation
Even an old person becomes young through constant mūlabandha. Pressing the yoni with part [of] the heel, one should contract the anus, while raising the apāna upwards: this is called mūlabandha.

Verses 75b to 77: Uddiyāna Bandha

उड्यानं कुरुते यस्मादविश्रान्तमहाखगः ।।७५।।

उड्डियानं तदेव स्यात्तत्र बन्धो विधीयते ।

उदरे पश्चिमं ताणं नाभेरुर्ध्वं तु कारयेत् ।।७६।।

उड्डियानोऽप्ययं बन्धो मृत्युमतङ्गकेसरी ।

बध्नाति हि शिरोजातमधोगामिनभोजलम् ।।७७।।

udyānaṃ kurute yasmādaviśrāntamahākhagaḥ (75b)
uddiyānaṃ tadeva syāttatra bandho vidhīyate
udare paścimaṃ tāṇaṃ nābherurdhvaṃ tu kārayet (76)
uddiyāno 'pyayaṃ bandho mṛtyumataṅgakesarī
badhnāti hi śirojātamadhogāminabhojalam (77)

Anvay

yasmāt: just like; *mahākhagaḥ*: great bird; *uddiyānam kurute*: flies upwards; *aviśrānta*: unwearied; *eva*: such; *syāt*: is; *uddiyānam*: *uddiyāna*; *tatra*: therefore; *vidhīyate*: it is considered; *bandhaḥ*: *bandha*; *kārayet*: one should put; *paścimam tāṇam*: western area; *udare*: of the stomach; *urdhvam*: above; *nābheḥ*: navel; *ayam*: this; *uddiyānah bandhaḥ*: *uddiyāna bandha*; *kesarī*: lion; *mataṅga*: elephant; *mṛtyu*: death; *Hi*: since; *badhnāti*: it binds; *jalam*: water; *śiro-jātam*: produced in the head; *adhogāmin*: flows down.

Translation

Just like the great bird [which] flies upwards unwearied, such is *uddiyāna.* Therefore it is considered a *bandha*. One should put the western area of the stomach above the navel. This *uddiyāna bandha* [is] a lion [to] the elephant [of] death, since it binds the water [which], produced in the head, flows down.

Verses 78 and 79a: Jālandhara bandha

ततो जालन्धरो बन्धः कर्मदुःखौघनाशनः ।

जालन्धरे कृते बन्धो कण्ठकोचलक्षणे ।।७८।।

न पीयूषं पतत्यग्नौ न च वायुः प्रधावति ।७९।

tato jālandharo bandhaḥ karmaduḥkhaughanāśanaḥ
jālandharo kṛte bandho kaṇṭhasaṃkocalakṣaṇe (78)
na pīyūṣaṃ patatyagnau na ca vāyuḥ pradhāvati (79a)

Anvay

tataḥ: in that way; *jālandharaḥ bandhaḥ*: jālandhara bandha; *nāśanaḥ*: destroys; *duḥkha*: suffering; *ogha*: multitude; *karma*: karmas; *jālandhare bandhaḥ kṛte*: when jālandhara bandha is performed; *lakṣaṇe*: indicated by; *saṃkoca*: contraction; *kaṇṭha*: throat; *pīyūṣam*: nectar; *na patati*: does not fall; *agnau*: in the fire; *na ca*: nor; *vāyuḥ*: *vāyu*, vital air; *pradhāvati*: does spread.

Translation

In that way *jālandhara bandha* destroys the suffering of a multitude of karmas. When jālandhara bandha is performed, indicated by contraction of the throat, nectar does not fall in the fire, nor does the *vāyu* spread.

Verses 79b to 82a: Results of Khecarī Mudrā

कपालकुहरे जिह्वा प्रविष्टा विपरीतगा ।।७९।।
भ्रुवोरन्तर्गता दृष्टिर्मुद्रा भवति खेचरी ।
न रोगो मरणं तस्य न निद्रा न क्षुधा तृषा ।।८०।।
न च मूर्च्छा भरेत्तस्य यो मुद्रां वेत्ति खेचरीम् ।
पीड्यते न च रोगेण लिप्यते न च कर्मणा ।।८१।।
बध्यते न च कालेन यस्य मुद्रास्ति खेचरी ।८२।

kapālakuhare jihvā praviṣṭā viparītagā (79b)
bhruvorantargatā dṛṣṭirmudrā bhavati khecarī
na rogo maraṇaṃ tasya na nidrā na kṣudhā tṛṣā (80)
na ca mūrcchā bharettasya yo mudrāṃ vetti khecarīm
pīḍyate na ca rogeṇa lipyate na ca karmaṇā (81)
badhyate na ca kālena yasya mudrāsti khecarī (82a)

Anvay

jihvā: tongue; *viparītagā*: inverted; *praviṣṭā*: enters; *kapāla-kuhare*: cave of the skull; *khecarī*: *khecarī*, 'moving in space'; *bhavati*: is; *dṛṣṭiḥ-mudrā*: mudrā of sight; *antargatā*: concealed; *bhruvoḥ*: in the eyebrow(s); *yaḥ*: whoever; *vetti*: knows; *tasya khecarīm mudrām*: about this khecarī mudrā; *bharet*: has; *na . . . na . . . ca*: neither . . . nor; *rogaḥ*: sickness; *maraṇam*: death; *nidrā*: sleep; *kṣudhā*: hunger; *tṛṣā*: thirst; *mūrcchā*: fainting; *yasya asti khecarī mudrā*: whoever does khecarī mudrā; *na . . . ca*: neither . . . nor; *pīḍyate*: is afflicted; *rogeṇa*: by disease; *lipyate*: bound; *karmaṇā*: to *karma*; *badhyate*: constrained; *kālena*: by time.

Translation

When the tongue, inverted, enters the cave of the skull, there is *khecarī*, the mudrā of sight concealed in the eyebrow [centre]. Whoever knows about this khecarī mudrā has neither sickness, nor death, nor sleep, nor hunger [or] thirst, nor fainting. Whoever does khecarī mudrā is neither afflicted by disease nor bound to *karma*, nor constrained by time.

Verses 82b to 86a: Khecarī Mudrā

चित्तं चरति खे यस्माज्जिह्वा भवति खेगता ।।८२।।
तेनैषा खेचरी नाम मुद्रा सिद्धनमस्कृता
खेचर्या मुद्रया यस्य लम्बिकोर्ध्वतः ।।८३।।
बिन्दुः क्षरति नो यस्य कामिन्यालिङ्गितस्य च ।
यावद्बिन्दुः स्थितो देहे तावन्मृत्युभयं कुतः ।।८४।।
यावद्बद्धा नभोमुद्रा तावद्बिन्दुर्न गच्छति ।
गलितोऽपि यदा बिन्दुः संप्राप्तो योनिमण्डले ।।८५।।
व्रजत्यूर्ध्वं हठाच्छक्त्या निबद्धो योनिमुद्रया ।८६।

cittaṃ carati khe yasmājjihvā bhavati khegatā (82b)
tenaiṣā khecarī nāma mudrā siddhanamaskṛtā
khecaryā mudrayā yasya lambikordhvataḥ (83b)
binduḥ kṣarati no yasya kāminyāliṅgitasya ca
yāvadbinduḥ sthito dehe tāvanmṛtyubhayaṃ kutaḥ (84)
yāvadbaddhā nabhomudrā tāvadbindurna gacchati
galito 'pi yadā binduḥ saṃprāpto yonimaṇḍale (85)
vrajatyūrdhvaṃ haṭhācchaktyā nibaddho yonimudrayā (86a)

Anvay

yasmāt: because; *cittam*: mind; *carati*: moves; *khe*: in space; *jihvā*: tongue; *bhavati khe-gatā*: has entered [this] space; *tena*: therefore; *eṣā mudrā*: this mudrā; *nāma khecarī*: of the name khecarī; *namaskṛtā*: is worshipped by; *siddha*: seers; *yasya*: when; *lambikā*: uvula; *ūrdhvataḥ*: upwards; *khecaryā mudrayā*: by khecarī mudrā; *binduḥ*: bindu; *no kṣarati*: does not flow down; *tasya*: even when; *āliṅgi*: in the embrace; *kāminī*: lovely woman; *kutaḥ*: where; *bhayam*: fear; *mṛtyu*: death; *yāvat . . . tāvat*: as long as; *binduḥ*: bindu; *sthitaḥ*: stays; *dehe*: in the body; *yāvat . . . tāvat*: as long as . . . then; *nabhomudrā*: khecarī mudrā; *baddhā*: is held; *binduḥ na gacchati*: bindu does not leave; *api yadā*: even when; *binduḥ saṃprāptaḥ*: bindu arrives; *yoni-maṇḍale*: at the ring of the yoni; *nibaddhaḥ*: contained there; *vrajati*: it travels; *ūrdhvam*: upwards; *haṭhāt-śaktyā*: through the forceful effort; *yoni-mudrayā*: of yoni mudrā.

Translation

Because the mind moves in space [and] the tongue has entered [this] space, therefore this mudrā of the name khecarī is worshipped by the seers. When the uvula [is pushed] upwards by khecarī mudrā, the bindu does not flow down, even when in the embrace [of] a lovely woman. Where is the fear [of] death, as long as the bindu stays in the body? As long as khecarī mudrā is held, then the bindu does not leave. Even when the bindu arrives at the ring of the yoni, contained there, it travels upwards through the forceful effort of yoni mudrā.

Verses 86b to 91a: Two kinds of bindu

स एव द्विविधो बिन्दुः पाण्डरो लोहितस्तथा ।।८६।।

पाण्डरं शुक्रमित्याहुर्लोहिताख्यं महारजः ।

विद्रुमद्रुमसंकाशं योनिस्थाना स्थितं रजः ।।८७।।

शशिस्थाने वसेद्विन्दुस्तयोरैक्यं सुदुर्लभम् ।

बिन्दुः शिवो रजः शक्तिर्बिन्दुरिन्दु रजो रविः ।।८८।।

उभयोः संगमादेव प्राप्यते परमं वपुः ।

वायुना शक्तिचालेन प्रेरितं खे यथा रजः ।।८९।।

रविणैकत्वमायाति भवेद्दिव्यं वपुस्तदा ।

शुक्लं चन्द्रेण संयुक्तं रजः सूर्यसमन्वितं ।।९०।।

द्वयोः समरसीभावं यो जानाति स योगवित् ।९१।

sa eva dvividho binduḥ pāṇḍaro lohitastathā (86b)
pāṇḍaraṃ śukramityāhurlohitākhyaṃ mahārajaḥ
vidrumadrumasaṃkāśaṃ yonisthāne sthitaṃ rajaḥ (87)
śaśisthāne vasedvindustayoraikyaṃ sudurlabham
binduḥ śivo rajaḥ śaktirbindurindu rajo raviḥ (88)
ubhayoḥ saṃgamādeva prāpyate paramaṃ vapuḥ
vāyunā śakticālena preritaṃ khe yathā rajaḥ (89)
raviṇaikatvamāyāti bhaveddivyaṃ vapustadā
śuklaṃ candreṇa saṃyuktaṃ rajaḥ sūryasamanvitam (90)
dvayoḥ samarasībhāvaṃ yo jānāti sa yogavit (91a)

Anvay

tathā: so; *sa binduḥ*: this bindu; *dvividhaḥ*: of two kinds; *pāṇḍaraḥ*: white; *lohitaḥ*: red; *pāṇḍaram*: white one; *iti āhuḥ*: is thus called; *śukram*: *śukra*, white, pure; *lohitaḥ*: red; *ākhyam*: is said; *mahā-rajaḥ*: much *rajas*, dynamism; *rajaḥ*: rajas; *sthitam*: located; *yoni- sthāne*: in the area of the yoni; *saṃkāśam*: looks like; *vidruma-druma*: column of coral; *vinduḥ vaset*: bindu remains ; *śaśi-sthāne*: in the seat of the moon; *aikyam*: union; *tayoḥ*: of these two; *sudurlabham*: very rare; *paramam vapuḥ*: highest form; *prāpyate*: can be reached; *saṃgamāt*: through the coming together; *ubhayoḥ*: of these two; *binduḥ śivaḥ rajaḥ*: Śiva energy [of] bindu; *raviḥ*: sun; *śaktiḥ-binduḥ-indu*: śakti energy of bindu [which is] the moon; *yathā*: when; *rajaḥ preritam*: rajas is directed; *khe*: heavenwards; *vāyunā śakti-cālena*: by the movement of the power of vāyu; *tadā*: then; *vapuḥ*: body; *āyāti*: approaching; *ekatvam*: unity; *raviṇa*: sun's eclipse; *bhavet*: becomes; *divyam*: divine; *śuklam*: *śukla*; *saṃyuktam*: is united; *candreṇa*: with the moon; *rajaḥ samanvitam*: rajas is connected with; *sūrya*: sun; *yaḥ jānāti*: whoever understands; *samarasībhāvam*: merging; *dvayoḥ*: of the two; *sa yogavit*: that person is a knower of yoga.

Translation

So this bindu [is] of two kinds, white [and] red. The white one is thus called *śukra* [and] the red is said [to have] much *rajas*. The rajas located in the area of the yoni looks like a column of coral. The bindu remains in the seat of the moon. The union of these two [is] very rare. The highest form can be reached through the coming together of these two: the Śiva energy [of] bindu [which is] the sun [and] the Śakti energy of bindu [which is] the moon. When rajas is directed heavenwards by the movement of the power of vāyu, then the body, approaching the unity [of] the sun's eclipse, becomes divine. *Śukla* is united with the moon; rajas is connected with the sun: whoever understands the merging of the two, that person is a knower of yoga.

Verses 91b to 93: Mahā Mudrā

शोधनं मलजालानां घटनं चन्द्रसूर्ययोः ।।९१।।

रसानां शोषणं सम्यङ्महामुद्राभिधीयते ।।९२।।

वक्षस्यस्तहनुर्निपीड्य सुषिरं योनेश्च वामाङ्घ्रिणा

हस्ताभ्यामनुधारयन्प्रविततं पादं तथा दक्षिणम् ।

आपूर्य श्वसनेन कुक्षियुगलं बध्वा शनै रेचयेदेषा पातकनाशिनी

ननु महामुद्रा नृणां प्रोच्यते ।।९३।।

śodhanaṃ malajālānāṃ ghaṭanaṃ candrasūryayoḥ (91b)
rasānāṃ śoṣaṇaṃ samyaṅmahāmudrābhidhīyate (92)
vakṣasyastahanurnipīḍya suṣiraṃ yoneśca vāmāṅghriṇā
hastābhyāmanudhārayanpravitataṃ pādaṃ tathā dakṣinam
āpūrya śvasanena kukṣiyugalaṃ badhvā śanai recayedeṣā
pātakanāśinī nanu mahāmudrā nṛṇāṃ procyate (93)

Anvay

śodhanam: cleansing; *mala-jālānām*: of waste matter; *ghaṭanam candra-sūryayoḥ*: union of the moon with the sun; *śoṣaṇam*: drying; *rasānām*: of fluids; *abhidhīyate*: is called; *samyak mahā-mudrā*: true mahā mudrā; *nipīḍya*: pressing down; *hanuḥ*: jaw; *vakṣasi*: on the chest; *ca*: and; *suṣiram*: hollow; *yoneḥ*: of the yoni; *vāma-aṅghriṇā*: with the left foot; *tathā*: then; *anudhārayan*: holding; *hastābhyām*: with both hands; *pravitatam*: stretched out; *dakṣinam*: right; *pādam*: leg; *āpūrya*: having filled; *kukṣi-yugalam*: whole abdomen; *śvasanena*: with the breath; *śanai*: slowly; *recayet*: one should exhale; *eṣā*: this; *nanu*: indeed; *mahā-mudrā*: mahā mudrā; *procyate*: said; *nāśinī*: to destroy; *pātaka*: sins; *nṛṇām*: of men.

Translation

The cleansing of waste matter, the union of the moon with the sun, the drying of fluids, [this] is called the true mahā mudrā. Pressing the jaw down on the chest, and the hollow of the yoni with the left foot, then holding with both hands the stretched out right leg, having filled the whole abdomen with the breath, one should slowly exhale. This [is] indeed the mahā mudrā, said to destroy the sins of men.

Verse 94: The Ātman

अथात्मनिर्णयं व्याख्यास्ये ।।
हृदिस्थाने अष्टदलपद्मं वर्तते तन्मध्ये रेखावलयं कृत्वा जीवात्मरूपं ज्योतीरूपमणुमात्रं वर्तते तस्मिन्सर्वं प्रतिष्ठितं भवति सर्वं जानाति सर्वं करोति सर्वमेतच्चरितमहं कर्ता ऽहं भोक्ता सुखी दुःखी काणः खञ्जो बधिरो मूकः कृशः स्थूलो ऽनेन प्रकारेण स्वतन्त्रवादेन वर्तते ।।
पूर्वदले विश्रमते पूर्वं दलं श्वेतवर्णं तदा भक्तिपुरःसरं धर्मे मतिर्भवति ।।
यदाऽग्नेयदले विश्रमते तदाग्नेयदलं रक्तवर्णं तदा निद्रालस्यमतिर्भवति ।।
यदा दक्षिणदले विश्रमते तद्ददक्षिणदलं कृष्णवर्णं तदा द्वेषकोपमतिर्भवति ।।
यदा नैरृतदले विश्रमति तन्नैरृतदलं नीलवर्णं तदा पापकर्महिंसामतिर्भवति ।।
यदा पश्चिमदले विश्रमते तत्पश्चिमदलं स्फटिकवर्णं तदा क्रीडाविनोदे मतिर्भवति ।।
यदा वायव्यदले विश्रमते वायव्यदलं माणिक्यवर्णं तदा गमनचलनवैरग्यमतिर्भवति ।।
यदुत्तरदले विश्रमते तदुत्तरदलं पीतवर्णं तदा सुखशृङ्गारमतिर्भवति ।।
यदेशानदले विश्रमते तदीशनदलं वैडूर्यवर्णं तदा दानादिकृपामतिर्भवति ।।

यदा संधिसंधिषु मतिर्भवति तदा
वातपित्तश्लेष्ममहाव्याधिप्रकोपो भवति ।।
यदा मध्ये तिष्ठति तदा सर्वं जानाति गायति नृत्यति
पठत्यानन्दं करोति ।।
यदा नेत्रश्रमो भवति श्रमनिर्भरणार्थं प्रथमरेखाबन्धूकपुष्पवर्णं
तदा निद्रावस्था भवति ।।
निद्रावस्थामध्ये स्वप्नावस्था भवति ।।
स्वप्नावस्थामध्ये दृष्टं श्रुतमनुमानसंभववार्ता इत्यादिकल्पनां
करोति तदादिश्रमो भवति ।।
श्रमनिर्हरणार्थं द्वितीयरेखावलयं कृत्वा मध्ये निमज्जनं कुरुते
द्वितीयरेखा इन्द्रकोपवर्णं तदा सुषुप्त्यवस्था भवति सुषुप्तौ
केवलपरमेश्चरसंबन्धिनी बुद्धिर्भवति नित्यबोधस्वरूपा भवति
पश्चात्परमेश्वरस्वरूपेण प्राप्तिर्भवति ।।
तृतीयरेखावलयं कृत्वा मध्ये निमज्जनं कुरुते तृतीयरेखा
पद्मरागवर्णं तदा तुरीयावस्था भवति तुरीये
केवलपरमात्मसंबन्धिनी भवति नित्यबोधस्वरूपा भवति तदा
शनैः शनैरुपरमेद्बुद्ध्या धृतिगृहीतयात्मसंस्थं मनः कृत्वा न
किंचिदपि चिन्तयेत्तदा प्राणापानयोरैक्यं कृत्वा सर्वं
विश्वमात्मस्वरूपेण लक्ष्यं धारयति ।
यदा तुरीयातीतावस्था तदा सर्वेषामानन्दस्वरूपो भवति
द्वन्द्वातीतो भवति यावद्देहधारणा वर्तते तावत्तिष्ठति
पश्चात्परमात्मस्वरूपेण प्राप्तिर्भवति इत्यनेन प्रकारेण मोक्षो
भवतीदमेवात्मदर्शनोपाया भवन्ति ।।
चतुष्पथसमायुक्तमहाद्वारकवायुना ।
सहस्थितत्रिकोणार्धगमने दृश्यते ऽच्युतः ।।९४।।

athātmaṇirnayaṃ vyākhyāsye.
hṛdisthāne aṣṭadalapadmaṃ vartate tanmadhye rekhāvalayaṃ kṛtvā jīvātmarūpam jyotīrūpamanumātraṃ vartate tasminsarvaṃ pratiṣṭhitaṃ bhavati sarvaṃ jānāti sarvaṃ karoti sarvametaccaritamahaṃ kartā 'haṃ bhoktā sukhī duḥkhī kānaḥ khañjo badhiro mūkaḥ kṛśaḥ sthūlo 'nena prakāreṇa svatantravādena vartate.
pūrvadale viśramate pūrvaṃ dalaṃ śvetavarṇaṃ tadā bhaktipuraḥsaraṃ dharme matirbhavati.
yadā 'gneyadale viśramate tadāgneyadalaṃ raktavarṇaṃ tadā nidrālasyamatirbhavati.
yadā dakṣinadale viśramate taddakṣinadalaṃ kṛṣṇavarṇaṃ tadā dveṣakopamatirbhavati.
yadā nairritadale viśramati tannairritadalaṃ nīlavarṇaṃ tadā pāpakarmahiṃsā - matirbhavati
yadā paścimadale viśramate tatpaścimadalaṃ sphaṭikavarṇaṃ tadā krīḍāvinode matirbhavati
yadā vāyavyadale viśramate vāyavyadalaṃ māṇikyavarṇaṃ tadā gamanacalanavairagya
matirbhavati
yaduttaradale viśramate taduttaradalaṃ pītavarṇaṃ tadā sukhaśriṅgāramatirbhavati
yadeśānadale viśramate tadīśanadalaṃ vaidūryavarṇaṃ tadā dānādikṛpāmatirbhavati
yadā saṃdhisaṃdhiṣu matirbhavati tadā vātapittaśleṣmamahāvyādhiprakopo bhavati
yadā madhye tiṣṭhati tadā sarvaṃ jānāti gāyati nṛtyati paṭhatyānandaṃ karoti
yadā netraśramo bhavati śramanirbharaṇārthaṃ prathamarekhābandhūkapuṣpavarṇaṃ tadā nidrāvasthā bhavati
nidrāvasthāmadhye svapnāvasthā bhavati
svapnāvasthāmadhye dṛṣṭaṃ śrutamanumānasaṃbhavavārtā ityādikalpanāṃ karoti tadādiśramo bhavati

śramanirharaṇārthaṃ dvitīyarekhāvalayaṃ kṛtvā madhye nimajjanaṃ kurute dvitīyarekhā indrakopavarṇaṃ tadā suṣuptyavasthā bhavati suṣuptau kevalaparameścarasaṃbandhinī buddhirbhavati nityabodhasvarūpā bhavati paścātparameśvarasvarūpeṇa prāptirbhavati
tṛtīyarekhāvalayaṃ kṛtvā madhye nimajjanaṃ kurute tṛtīyarekhā padmarāgavarṇaṃ tadā turīyāvasthā bhavati turīye kevalaparamātmasaṃbandhinī bhavati nityabodhasvarūpā bhavati tadā śanaiḥ śanairuparamedbuddhyā dhṛtigṛhītayātmasaṃsthaṃ manaḥ kṛtvā na kiṃcidapi cintayettadā prāṇāpānayoraikyaṃ kṛtvā sarvaṃ viśvamātmasvarūpeṇa lakṣyaṃ dhārayati;
yadā turīyātītāvasthā tadā sarveṣāmānandasvarūpo bhavati dvandvātīto bhavati yāvaddehadhāraṇā vartate tāvattiṣṭhati paścātparamātmasvarūpeṇa prāptirbhavati ityanena prakāreṇa mokṣo bhavatīdamevātmadarśaṇopāyā bhavanti.
catuṣpathasamāyuktamahādvārakavāyunā;
sahasthitatrikonārdhagamane dṛśyate 'cyutaḥ (94)

Anvay

atha: now; *vyākhyāsye nirṇayam*: I shall describe in detail; *ātma*: atman, Real Self; *hṛdi-sthāne*: in the seat of the heart; *vartate*: is; *padmam*: lotus; *aṣṭa-dala*: eight petals; *tat-madhye*: in its centre; *vartate*: abides; *jīvātmarūpam*: *jīvātman*, individual soul; *jyotī-rūpam*: in the form of a bright light; *anu-mātram*: atomic in size; *rekhāvalayam kṛtvā*: shaped as a circle; *tasmin*: in it; *bhavati pratiṣṭhitam*: is placed; *sarvam*: everything; *jānāti sarvam*: it knows everything; *karoti sarvam*: it does everything; *caritam etat*: it behaves thus; *aham kartā*: I am the doer; *aham bhoktā*: I am the enjoyer; *sukhī*: happy; *duḥkhī*: sad; *kānaḥ*: one-eyed; *khañjaḥ*: lame; *badhiraḥ*: deaf; *mūkaḥ*: mute; *kṛśaḥ*: thin; *sthūlaḥ*: stout; *anena prakāreṇa*: in this way; *vartate*: it exists; *svatantravādena*: independently; *viśramate*: it rests; *pūrva-dale*: on the eastern petal; *śveta-varṇam*: white colour; *tadā*:

then; *matirbhavati*: it is inclined; *dharme*: to righteousness; *bhakti-puraḥsaram*: together with devotion; *yadā*: when; *agneya-dale*: on the south-eastern petal; *rakta*: red; *nidrā*: sleep; *ālasya*: sloth; *dakṣina-dale*: on the southern petal; *kṛṣṇa-varṇam*: black colour; *matirbhavati*: it is prone to; *dveṣa*: hatred; *kopa*: anger; *nairrita-dale*: on the south-western petal; *nīla-varṇam*: blue colour; *pāpa-karma-hiṃsā*: sinful [and] violent actions; *paścima-dale*: on the western petal; *sphaṭika-varṇam*: crystal colour; *matirbhavati*: it is inclined to; *krīḍā-vinode*: play [and] entertainment; *vāyavya-dale*: on the north-western petal; *māṇikya-varṇam*: ruby colour; *gamana*: walking; *calana*: wandering; *vairagya*: detachment; *yad . . . tad*: whenever . . . then; *uttara-dale*: on the northern petal; *pīta-varṇam*: yellow colour; *matirbhavati*: its mind is; *sukha*: happy; *śriṅgāra*: loving; *īśāna-dale*: on the north-eastern petal; *vaidūrya-varṇam*: lapis lazuli, deep celestial blue; *kṛpā*: compassion; *dāna-ādi*: donations etc; *matirbhavati*: it settles; *saṃdhisaṃdhiṣu*: on the junctures; *bhavati*: there is; *mahāvyādhi*: severe disease; *vāta*: wind; *pittaśleṣma*: bile phlegm; *tiṣṭhati*: it stays; *madhye*: in the middle; *jānāti*: it knows; *sarvam*: everything; *gāyati*: sings; *nṛtyati*: dances; *paṭhati*: recites; *karoti ānandam*: is blissful; *netra*: eye; *bhavati*: is; *śramaḥ*: in pain; *śrama-nirbharaṇa-artham*: in order to remove the pain; *prathama*: first; *rekhā*: outline; *bandhūka-puṣpa-varṇam*: colour [of] the bandhuka flower (bright red); *bhavati nidrā-avasthā*: goes into the state of sleep; *svapnā-avasthā-madhye*: in the midst of the dreaming state; *karoti*: it creates; *kalpanām*: ideas; *vārtā*: relating to; *dṛṣṭam*: perception; *śrutam*: memory; *anumāna*: possibility; *iti*: words; *ādi*: and so on; *tadā bhavati*: then there is; *śramaḥ ādi*: pain etc; *śrama-nirharaṇa-artham*: in order to have the pain removed; *kṛtvā*: having made; *dvitīya-rekhā-valayam*: second circular line; *kurute nimajjanam*: it sinks; *madhye*: in the middle; *dvitīya-rekhā*: second circle; *indrakopa-varṇam*: colour of the insect Indragopa; *tadā bhavati*: then there is; *suṣupti-avasthaa*: state of deep sleep.

suṣuptau: in deep sleep; *bhavati buddhiḥ*: there is one thought; *saṃbandhinī*: relates to; *parameśvara kevala*: Supreme Being alone; *bhavati svarūpā*: has the quality; *nitya-bodha*: eternal wisdom; *prāptiḥ bhavati*: it attains; *paścāt*: later; *svarūpeṇa*: through the nature; *parameśvara*: Supreme Being; *kṛtvā*: having made; *tṛtīya-rekhā-valayam*: third circular line; *kurute nimajjanam*: it sinks; *madhye*: in the middle; *tṛtīya-rekhā*: third circle; *padmarāga-varṇam*: ruby colour; *tadā bhavati*: then comes; *turīyā-avasthā*: fourth state; *turīye*: in the fourth; *bhavati*: there is; *saṃbandhinī*: connection with; *paramātma*: Supreme Spirit; *kevala*: alone; *bhavati*: becoming; *nityabodha-svarūpā*: nature of eternal wisdom; *tadā*: then; *śanaiḥ śanaiḥ*: gradually; *uparamet*: one should await; *buddhyā*: of *buddhi*; *dhṛti-gṛhītayā*: with constancy and resolution; *kṛtvā saṃstham*: having contained; *manaḥ*: mind; *cintayet*: one should think of; *na kiṃcidapi*: nothing else; *prāṇa-apānayoḥ-aikyam kṛtvā*: having united prāṇa and apāna; *dhārayati*: one focuses on; *lakṣyam*: aim; *sarvaṃ viśvam*: whole universe; *ātmasvarūpeṇa*: through the nature of the atman; *yadā*: when; *turīya-atīta-avasthā*: state beyond the fourth; *tadā*: then; *bhavati svarūpaḥ*: one experiences; *sarveṣām*: everything; *ānanda*: bliss; *bhavati*: is; *dvandvātītaḥ*: beyond duality; *tiṣṭhati*: one stays; *yāvat . . . tāvat*: as long as; *vartate*: there is; *deha-dhāraṇā*: wearing of the body; *paścāt*: next; *prāptiḥ bhavati*: one attains; *svarūpeṇa*: nature; *paramātma*: Supreme Spirit; *anena prakāreṇa*: through this means; *bhavati mokṣaḥ*: there is liberation; *upāyāḥ*: approaches; *darśana*: knowing; *ātma*: atman, Supreme Self; *bhavanti*: are; *eva*: surely; *idam*: this.

acyutaḥ: Imperishable One; *dṛśyate*: is seen; *vāyunā*: through the breath; *gamane*: entering; *mahādvāraka*: great hole; *catuṣ-patha*: four paths; *samāyukta*: meet; *ardha trikona*: half triangle; *sahasthita*: abide together.

Translation

Now I shall describe in detail the ātman. In the seat of the heart is a lotus [with] eight petals. In its centre abides the *jīvātman* in the form of a bright light, atomic in size [and] shaped as a circle. In it is placed everything. It knows everything. It does everything. It behaves thus: I am the doer. I am the enjoyer. [I am] happy, sad, one-eyed, lame, deaf, mute, thin, stout. In this way it exists independently.

[When] it rests on the eastern petal [which is] white [in] colour, then it is inclined to righteousness together with devotion. When it rests on the south-eastern petal [which is] red [in] colour, then it is inclined to sleep [and] sloth. When it rests on the southern petal [which is] black [in] colour, then it is prone to hatred [and] anger. When it rests on the south-western petal [which is] blue [in] colour, then it is prone to sinful [and] violent actions. When it rests on the western petal [which is of] a crystal colour, then it is inclined to play [and] entertainment. When it rests on the north-western petal [which is of] a ruby colour, then it is inclined to walking, wandering [and] detachment. Whenever it rests on the northern petal [which is] yellow [in] colour, then its mind is happy [and] loving. When it rests on the north-eastern petal [which is] a deep, celestial blue, then it is inclined to compassion [and] donations etc. When it settles on the junctures [of the petals], then there is severe disease [due to] an excess of wind, bile [or] phlegm. When it stays in the middle, then it knows everything, sings, dances, recites [and] is blissful. When the eye is in pain, in order to remove the pain [it makes] first an outline the colour [of] the bandhuka flower, then goes into the state of sleep. In the middle of the sleeping state is the dreaming state. In the midst of the dreaming state it creates the ideas relating to perception, memory, possibility, words and so on. Then there is pain etc. In order to have the pain removed, having made a second circular line, it sinks in the middle. The second circle is the colour of the insect Indragopa.

In deep sleep there is one thought [which] relates to the Supreme Being alone. [This state] has the quality [of] eternal wisdom, [which] it attains later through the nature [of] the Supreme Being. Having made a third circular line, it sinks in the middle. The third circle [is] a ruby colour. Then comes the fourth state. In the fourth state there is connection with the Supreme Spirit alone, becoming the nature of eternal wisdom. Then one should gradually await [the intuition] of *buddhi* with constancy and resolution. Having contained the mind [in] the ātman, one should think of nothing else. Having united prāṇa and apāna, one focuses one's aim on the whole universe through the nature of the atman. When [one is in] the state beyond the fourth, then one experiences everything [as] bliss [and] is beyond duality. One stays there as long as there is wearing of the body. Next one attains the nature [of] the Supreme Spirit. Through this means there is liberation. The approaches to knowing the ātman are surely this.

The Imperishable One is seen through the breath, entering the great hole [where] four paths meet, [and] the half triangle [which] abide together.

Verses 95 to 97a: Meditating on the bīja mantras of the five elements

पूर्वोक्तत्रिकोणस्थानादुपरि पृथिव्यादिपञ्चवर्णकं ध्येयम् ।
प्राणादिपञ्चवायुश्च बीजं वर्णं च स्थानकम् ।
यकारं प्राणबीजं च नीलजीमूतसन्निभम् ।
रखारमग्निबीजं च अपानादित्यसंनिभम् ।।९५।।
लकारं पृथिवीरूपं व्यानं बन्धूकसंनिभम् ।
वकारं जीवबीजं च उदानं शङ्खवर्णकम् ।।९६।।
हकारं वियत्स्वरूपं च समानं स्फटिकप्रभम् ।९७।

pūrvoktatrikonasthānādupari pṛthivyādipañcavarṇakaṃ dhyeyam
prāṇādipañcavāyuśca bījaṃ varṇaṃ ca sthānakam
yakāraṃ prāṇabījaṃ ca nīlajīmūtasannibham
rakhāramagnibījaṃ ca apānādityasaṃnibham (95)
lakāraṃ pṛthivīrūpaṃ vyānaṃ bandhūkasaṃnibham
vakāraṃ jīvabījaṃ ca udānaṃ śaṅkhavarṇakam (96)
hakāraṃ viyatsvarūpaṃ ca samānaṃ sphaṭikaprabham (97a)

Anvay

upari sthānāt: above the area; *pūrvokta-trikona*: aforesaid triangle; *dhyeyam*: one should meditate on; *pañca-varṇakam*: five letters; *pṛthivī*: earth; *ādi*: and the other(s); *pañca-vāyuḥ*: five vital airs; *prāṇa-ādi*: prāṇa etc; *ca*: and; *varṇam*: colour; *sthānakam*: position; *bījam*: seeds; *yakāram*: letter ya; *prāṇa-bījam*: seed of prāṇa; *ca sannibham*: and resembles; *nīla-jīmūta*: blue cloud; *rakhāram*: letter ra; *agni-bījam*: seed of agni; *ca saṃnibham*: and resembles; *āditya*: sun; *lakāram*: letter la; *pṛthivī-rūpam*: form of *pṛthivī*; *vyānam*: vyāna; *bandhūka-saṃnibham*: resembling the bandhuka flower; *vakāram*: letter va; *jīva-bījam*: seed of jīva; *udānam*: udāna; *ca*: and; *śaṅkha-varṇakam*: colour of a conch; *hakāram*:

letter ha; *viyat-svarūpam*: form of *ākāśa; samānam*: samāna; *sphaṭika-prabham*: radiance of crystal.

Translation

Above the area [of] the aforesaid triangle, one should meditate on the five letters [of] earth and the other [elements], the five vital airs [of] prāṇa etc, and the colour and position [of their] seeds. The letter *ya* [is] the seed of prāṇa, and resembles a blue cloud. The letter *ra* [is] the seed of agni, [is of the vital air] apāna, and resembles the sun. The letter *la*, the form of *pṛthivi*, [is of] vyāna, resembling the bandhuka flower. The letter *va* [is] the seed of jīva [of] udāna, and the colour of a conch. The letter *ha* [is] the form of *ākāśa*, [of] samāna, and [has] the radiance of crystal.

Verses 97b to 99a: One jīva

हृन्नाभिनासाकर्णं च पादाङ्गुष्ठादिसंस्थितम् ।।९७।।
द्विसप्ततिसहस्राणि नाडीमार्गेषु वर्तते ।
अष्टाविंशतिकोटीषु रोमकूपेषु संस्थिताः ।।९८।।
समानप्राण एकस्तु जीवः स एक एव हि ।९९।

hṛnnābhināsākarṇaṃ ca pādāṅguṣṭhādisaṃsthitam (97b)
dvisaptatisahasrāṇi nāḍīmārgeṣu vartate
aṣṭāviṃśatikoṭīṣu romakūpeṣu saṃsthitāḥ (98)
samānaprāṇa ekastu jīvaḥ sa eka eva hi (99a)

Anvay

saṃsthitam: located in; *hṛt*: heart; *nābhi*: navel; *nāsā*: nose; *karṇam*: ears; *pāda*: feet; *ca*: and; *aṅguṣṭha*: fingers; *ādi*: etc; *vartate*: flow; *dvisaptatisahasrāṇi nāḍī-mārgeṣu*: in the seventy-two thousand nāḍīs; *saṃsthitāḥ*: are; *aṣṭāviṃśatikoṭīṣu roma-kūpeṣu*: in the two hundred and eighty million hair-pores; *tu*: yet; *ekaḥ samāna-prāṇa*: one and the same energy; *sa*: this; *eva hi*: indeed; *eka jīvaḥ*: one jīva.

Translation

[The vital energies] located in the heart, navel, nose, ears, feet and fingers etc flow in the seventy-two thousand nāḍīs, are in the two hundred and eighty million hair-pores, [and] yet [is] one and the same energy. This [is] indeed the one jīva.

Verses 99b to 105: Praṇava

रेचकादि त्रयं कुर्याद्दृढचित्तः समाहितः ।।९९।।
शनैः समस्तमाकृष्य हृत्सरोरुहकोटरे ।
प्राणापानौ च बद्ध्वा तु प्रणवेन समुच्चरेत् ।।१००।।
कर्णसंकोचनं कृत्वा लिङ्गसंकोचनं तथा
मूलाधारात्सुषुम्ना च पद्मतन्तुनिभा सुभा ।।१०१।।
अमूर्तो वर्तते नादो वीणादण्डसमुत्थितः ।
शङ्खनादादिभिश्चैव मध्यमेव ध्वनिर्यथा ।।१०२।।
व्योमरन्ध्रगतो नादो मायूरं नादमेव च ।
कपालकुहरे मध्ये चतुर्द्वारस्य मध्यमे ।।१०३।।
तदात्मा राजते तत्र यथा व्योम्नि दिवाकरः ।
कोदण्डद्वयमध्ये तु ब्रह्मरन्ध्रेशक्त्या च ।।१०४।।
स्वात्मानं पुरुषं पश्येन्मनस्तत्र लयं गतम् ।
रत्नानि ज्योत्स्निनादं तु बिन्दुमाहेश्वरं पदम् ।
य एवं वेद पुरुषः स कैवल्यं समश्नुत इत्युपनिषत् ।।१०५।।

recakādi trayaṃ kuryāddṛḍhacittaḥ samāhitaḥ (99b)
śanaiḥ samastamākṛṣya hṛtsaroruhakoṭare
prāṇāpānau ca baddhvā tu praṇavena samuccaret (100)
karṇasaṃkocanaṃ kṛtvā liṅgasaṃkocanaṃ tathā
mūlādhārātsuṣumnā ca padmatantunibhā subhā (101)
amūrto vartate nādo vīṇādaṇḍasamutthitaḥ
śaṅkhanādādibhiścaiva madhyameva dhvaniryathā (102)
vyomarandhragato nādo māyūraṃ nādameva ca
kapālakuhare madhye caturdvārasya madhyame (103)
tadātmā rājate tatre yathā vyomni divākaraḥ
kodaṇḍadvayamadhye tu brahmarandhreśaktyā ca (104)
svātmānaṃ puruṣaṃ paśyenmanastatra layaṃ gatam
ratnāni jyotsninādaṃ tu bindumāheśvaraṃ padam

ya evaṃ veda puruṣaḥ sa kaivalyaṃ samaśnuta ityupaniṣat (105)

Anvay

dṛḍha: strong; *samāhitaḥ*: concentrated; *cittaḥ*: mind; *kuryāt*: one should do; *trayam*: three; *recaka-ādi*: exhalation etc; *śanaiḥ*: slowly; *ākṛṣya*: drawing in; *samastam*: whole; *ca*: and; *kṛtvā saṃkocanam*: contracting; *karṇa*: throat; *liṅga*: genital organ; *baddhvā*: joining together; *prāṇa-apānau*: prāṇa and apāna; *koṭare*: in the cave; *saroruha*: lotus; *hṛt*: heart; *samuccaret*: one should chant; *praṇavena*: praṇava. *mūlādhārāt*: from mūlādhāra; *vartate*: is; *suṣumnā*: suṣumnā; *nibhā*: resembling; *subhā tantu*: radiant thread; *padma*: lotus; *amūrtaḥ nādaḥ*: subtle nāda; *samutthitaḥ*: rises up; *vīṇādaṇḍa*: spinal column; *ca*: and; *yathā dhvaniḥ*: its sound; *madhyam*: middle; *iva*: like; *śaṅkhanāt-ādibhiḥ*: of a conch etc; *gataḥ*: it enters; *randhra*: opening; *vyoma*: ether; *nādam*: sound; *eva*: that of; *māyūram*: peacock; *madhye*: in the middle; *kuhare*: cavity; *kapāla*: skull; *madhyame*: between; *catuḥ-dvārasya*: four doors; *rājate*: shines; *tat ātmā*: the ātman; *tatra yathā*: just like; *divākaraḥ*: sun; *vyomni*: in the sky; *tu*: then; *madhye*: between; *dvaya kodaṇḍa*: two bows; *brahmarandhre*: in the fontanelle; *paśyet*: one sees; *puruṣam śaktyā*: puruṣa with shakti; *sva-ātmānam*: one's own ātman; *tatra*: there; *manaḥ*: individual mind; *gatam layam*: becomes absorbed; *sa puruṣaḥ*: that person; *samaśnuta*: attains; *kaivalyam*: final liberation; *yaḥ*: who; *veda*: understands; *ratnāni*: gems; *jyotsni*: moonlight; *nādam*: nāda; *bindu*: bindu; *padam māheśvaram*: seat of Maheśvara; *iti upaniṣat*: thus speaks the Upaniṣad.

Translation

[With] a strong [and] concentrated mind, one should do the three: exhalation etc. Slowly drawing in the whole [breath] and contracting the throat [and] genital organ, joining together prāṇa and apāna in the cave [of] the lotus [of] the heart, one should chant the praṇava. From mūlādhāra is suṣumnā, resembling the radiant thread [of] the lotus. The subtle nāda rises up the spinal column, and its sound [from] the middle [is] like [that] of a conch etc. [When] it enters the opening [of] the ether, the sound is that of a peacock. In the middle [of] the cavity [of] the skull between the four doors, shines the ātman, just like the sun in the sky. Then between the two bows in the fontanelle, one sees puruṣa with śakti [as] one's own ātman. There the individual mind becomes absorbed. That person attains final liberation who understands gems, moonlight, nāda, bindu [and] the seat of Maheśvara. Thus speaks the Upaniṣad.

इति ध्यानबिन्दूपनिषत्समाप्ता ॥

iti dhyānabindūpaniṣatsamāptā

Anvay

iti samāptā: thus concludes; *dhyānabindu-upaniṣat*: Dhyānabindu Upaniṣad.

Translation

Thus concludes the Dhyānabindu Upaniṣad.

Appendices

1. Sanskrit

ध्यात्वा यद्ब्रह्ममात्रं ते स्वावशेषधिया ययुः ।
योगतत्त्वज्ञानफलं तत्स्वमात्रं विचिन्तये ।।
ॐ सह नाववत्विति शान्तिः ।।

यदि शैलसं पापं विस्तीर्णं बहुयोजनम् ।
भिद्यते ध्यानयोगेन नान्यो भेदः कदाचन ।।१।।

बीजाक्षरं परं बिन्दुं नादं तस्योपरि स्थितम् ।
सशब्दं चाक्षरे क्षीणे निःशब्दं परं पदम् ।।२।।

अनाहतं तु यच्छब्दं तस्य शब्दस्य यत्परं ।
तत्परं बिन्दते यस्तु स योगी छिन्नसंशयः ।।३।।

वालाग्रशतसाहस्रं तस्य भागस्य भागिनः ।
तस्य भागस्य भागार्धं तत्क्षये तु निरञ्जनम् ।।४।।

पुष्पमध्ये यथा गन्धः पयोमध्ये यथा घृतम् ।
तिलमध्ये यथा तैलं पापाणेष्विव काञ्चनम् ।।५।।
एवं सर्वाणि भूतानि मणौ सूत्र इवात्मनि ।
स्थिरबुद्धिरसंसूढो ब्रह्मविद्ब्रह्मणि स्थितः ।।६।।
तिलानां तु यथा तैलं पुष्पे गन्ध इवाश्रितः ।

पुरुषस्य शरीरे तु सबाह्याभ्यन्तरे स्थितः ।।७।।

वृक्षं तु सकलं विद्याच्छाया तस्यैव निष्कला ।
सकले निष्कले भावे सर्वत्रात्मा व्यवस्थितः ।।८।।

ओमित्येकाक्षरं ब्रह्म ध्येयं सर्वमुमुक्षुभिः ।९।

पृथिव्यग्निश्च ऋग्वेदो भूरित्येव पितामहः ।।९।।
अकारे तु लयं प्राप्ते प्रथमे प्रणवांशके ।
अन्तरिक्षं यजुर्वायुर्भुवो विष्णुर्जनार्दनः ।।१०।।
उकारे तु लयं प्राप्ते द्वितीये प्रणवांशके ।
द्यौः सूर्यः सामवेदश्च स्वरित्येव महेश्वरः ।।११।।
मकारे तु लयं प्राप्ते तृतीये प्रणवांशके ।
अकारः पीतवर्णः स्याद्रजोगुण उदीरितः ।।१२।।
उकारः सात्त्विकः शुक्लो मकारः कृष्णतामसः ।१३।
अष्टाङ्ग च चतुष्पादं त्रिस्थानं पञ्चदैवतम् ।।१३।।
ओंकार यो न जानाति ब्रह्मणो न भवेत्तु सः
प्रणवो धनुः शरो ह्यात्मा ब्रह्म तल्लक्ष्यमुच्यते ।।१४।।
अप्रमत्तेन वेद्धव्यं शरवत्तन्मयो भवेत् ।
निवर्तन्ते क्रियाः सर्वास्तस्मिन्दृष्टे परावरे ।।१५।।

ओंकारप्रभवा देवा ओंकारप्रभवाः स्वराः ।
ओंकारप्रभवं सर्वं त्रैलोक्यं सचराचरम् ।।१६।।
ह्रस्वो दहति पापानि दीर्घः संपत्प्रदो ऽव्ययः ।
अर्धमात्रासमा युक्तः प्रणवो मोक्षदातक्तः ।।१७।।

तैलधारामिवाच्छिन्नं दीर्घघण्टानिनादवत् ।
अवाच्यं प्रणवस्याग्रं यस्तं वेद स वेदवित् ।।१८।।
हृत्पद्भकर्णिकामध्ये स्थिरदीपनिभाकृतिं ।
अङ्गुष्ठमात्रमचलं ध्यायेदोंकारमीश्वरम् ।।१९।।

इडया वायुमापूर्य पूरयित्वोदरस्थितं ।
ओंकारं देहमध्यस्थं ध्यायेज्ज्वालावलीवृतम् ।।२०।।
ब्रह्मा पूरक इत्युक्तो विष्णुः कुम्भक उच्यते ।
रेचो रुद्र इति प्रोक्तः प्राणायामस्य देवताः ।।२१।।
आत्मानमरणिं कृत्वा प्रणवं चोत्तरारणिम् ।
ध्याननिर्मथनाभ्यासादेव पश्येन्निगूढवत् ।।२२।।
ओंकारध्वनिनादेन वायोः संहरणान्तिकम् ।
यावद्वलं समादध्यात्सम्यङ्नादलयावधि ।।२३।।
गमागमस्थं गमनादिशून्यमोंकारमेकं रविकोटिदीप्तिम् ।
पश्यन्ति ये सर्वजनान्तरस्थं हंसात्मकं ते विरजा भवन्ति
।।२४।।
यन्मनस्त्रिजगात्सृष्टिस्थितिव्यसनकर्मकृत् ।
तन्मनो विलयं याति तद्विष्णोः परम पदम् ।।२५।।

अष्टपत्रं तु हृत्पद्मं द्वात्रंशत्केसरानिवितम् ।
तस्य मध्ये स्थितो भानुर्भानुमध्यगतः शशी ।।२६।।
शशिमध्यगतो वह्निर्वह्निमध्यगता प्रभा ।
प्रभामध्यगतं पीठं नानारत्नप्रवेष्टितम् ।।२७।।
तस्य पीठमध्यगतं वासुदेवं निरञ्जनम् ।
श्रीवत्सकौस्तुभोरस्कं मुक्तामणिविभूषितम् ।।२८।।

शुद्धस्फटिकसंकाशं चन्द्रकोटिसमप्रभम् ।
एवं ध्यायेन्महाविष्णुमेवं वा विनयान्वितः ।।२९।।

अतसीपुष्पसंकाशं नाभिस्थाने प्रतिष्ठितम् ।
चतुर्भुजं महाविष्णुं पूरकेण विचिन्तयेत् ।।३०।।
कुम्भकेन हृदि स्थाने चिन्तयेत्कमलासनम् ।
ब्रह्माणं रक्तगौराभं चतुर्वक्रं पितामहम् ।।३१।।
रेचकेन तु विद्यात्मा ललाटस्थं त्रिलोचनम् ।
शुद्धस्फटिकसंकाशं निष्कलं पापनाशनम् ।।३२।।
अन्नपत्रमधःपुष्पमूर्ध्वनालमधोमुखम् ।
कदलीपुष्पसंकाशं सर्ववेदमयं शिवम् ।।३३।।
शतारं शतपत्राढयं विकीर्णाम्बुजकर्णिकम् ।
तत्रार्कचन्द्रवह्नीनामुपर्यु - परिचिन्तयेत् ।।३४।।
पद्मस्योद्धाटनं कृत्वा बोधचन्द्राग्निसूर्यकम् ।
तस्य हृद्वीजमाहृत्य आत्मानं चरते ध्रुवम् ।।३५।।

त्रिस्थानं च त्रिमात्रं च त्रिब्रह्म च त्रयाक्षरम् ।
त्रिमात्रमर्धमात्रं वा यस्तं वेद स वेदवित् ।।३६।।
तैलधारामिवाच्छिन्नदीर्घघण्टानिनादवत् ।
बिन्दुनादकलातीतं यस्तं वेद स वेदवित् ।।३७।।

यथैवोत्पलनालेन तोयमाकर्षयेन्नरः ।
तथैवोत्कर्षयेद्वायुं योगी योगपथे स्थितः ।।३८।।
अर्धमात्रात्पकं कृत्वा कोशीभूतं तु पङ्कजम् ।
कर्षयेन्नालमात्रेण भ्रुवोर्मध्ये लयं नयेत् ।।३९।।

भ्रुवोर्मध्ये ललाटे तु नासिकायास्तु मूलतः ।
जानीयादमृतं स्थानं तद्ब्रह्मायतनं महत् ।।४०।।

आसनानि प्राणसंरोधः प्रत्याहारश्च धारणा ।
ध्यानं समाधिरेतानि योगाङ्गानि भवन्ति षट् ।।४१।।

आसनानि च तावन्ति यावन्त्यो जीवजातयः ।
एतेषामतुलान्भेदा न्विजानाति महेश्वरः ।।४२।।
सिद्धं भद्रं तथा सिम्हं पद्मं चेति चतुष्टयम् ।४३।

आधारं प्रथमं चक्रं स्वाधिष्ठानं द्वितीयकम् ।।४३।।
योनिस्थानं तयोर्मध्ये कामरूप निगद्यते ।
आधाराख्ये गुदस्थाने पङ्कजं यच्चतुर्दलम् ।।४४।।
तन्मध्ये प्रोच्यते योनिः कामाख्या सिद्धवन्दिता ।
योनिमध्ये स्थितं लिङ्गं पश्चिमाभिमुखं तथा ।।४५।।
मस्तके मणिवभ्दिन्नं यो जानाति स योगवित्
तप्तचामीकराकारं तडिल्लेखेव विस्फुरत् ।।४६।।
चतुरस्रमुपर्यग्नेरधो मेढ्रात्प्रतिष्ठितम्
स्वशब्देन भवेत्प्राणः स्वाधिष्ठानं तदाश्रयम् ।।४७।।
स्वादिष्ठानं ततश्चक्रं मेढ्रमेव निगद्यते
मणिवत्तन्तुना यत्र वायुना पूरितं वपुः ।।४८।।
तन्नाभिमण्डलं चक्रं प्रोच्यते मणिपूरकं ।
द्वादशारमहाचक्रे पुण्यपापनियन्त्रितः ।।४९।।
तावज्जीवो भ्रमत्येवं यावत्तत्त्वं न विन्दति ।५०।

ऊर्ध्वं मेढ्रादधो नाभेः कन्दो यो ऽस्ति खगाण्डवत् ।।५०।।
तत्र नाड्यः समुत्पन्नाः सहस्राणि द्विसप्ततिः ।
तेषु नाडीसहस्रेषु द्विसप्ततिरुदाहृताः ।।५१।।
प्रधानाः प्राणवाहिन्यो भूयस्तत्र दश स्मृताः ।
इडा च पिङ्गला चैव सुषुम्ना च तृतीयका ।।५२।।
गाम्धारी हस्तिजिह्वा च पूषा चैव यशस्विनी ।
अलम्बुसा कुहूरत्र शङ्खिनी दशमी स्मृता ।।५३।।

एवं नाडीमयं चक्रं विज्ञेयं योगिना सदा ।
सततं प्राणवाहिन्यः सोमसूर्याग्निदेवताः ।।५४।।
इडापिङ्गलासुषुम्नास्तिस्रो नाड्यः प्रकीर्तिताः ।
इडा वामे स्थिता भागे पिङ्गला दक्षिणे स्थिता ।।५५।।
सुषुम्ना मध्यदेशे तु प्राणमार्गास्त्रयः स्मृताः ।
प्राणो ऽपानः समानश्चोदानो व्यानस्तथैव च ।।५६।।
नागः कूर्मः कृकरको देवदत्तो धनंजयः ।
प्राणादाः पञ्च विख्याता नागाद्याः पञ्च वायवः ।।५७।।
एते नाडीसहस्रेषु वर्तन्ते जीवरूपिणः ।५८।

प्राणापानवशो जीवो ह्यधश्चोर्ध्वं प्रधावति ।।५८।।
वामदक्षिणमार्गेण चन्चलत्वान्न दृश्यते ।
आक्षिप्तो भुजदण्डेन यथोच्चलति कन्दुका ।।५९।।
प्राणापानसमाक्षिप्तस्तद्वज्जीवो न विश्रमेत् ।
अपानात्कर्षति प्राणो ऽपानः प्राणाच्च कर्षति ।।६०।।
खगरज्जुवदित्येतद्यो जानाति स योगवित् ।६१।

हकारेण बहिर्याति सकारेण विशेत्पुनः ।।६१।।
हंसहंसेत्यमुं मन्त्रं जीवो जपति सर्वदा ।
शतानि षट्दिवारात्रं सहस्राण्येकविंशतिः ।।६२।।
एतत्संख्यान्वितं मन्त्रं जीवो जपति सर्वदा ।
अजपा नाम गायत्री योगिनां मोक्षदा सदा ।।६३।।
अस्याः संकल्पमात्रेण नरः पापैः प्रमुच्यते ।
अनया सदृशी विद्या अनया सदृशो जपः ।।६४।।
अनया सदृशं पुण्यं न भूतं न भविष्यति ।६५।

येन मार्गेण गन्तव्यं ब्रह्मस्थानं निरामयम् ।।६५।।
मुखेनाच्छाद्य तद्द्वारं प्रसुप्ता परमेश्वरी ।
प्रबुद्धा वह्नियोगेन मनसा मरुता सह ।।६६।।
सूचिवद्गुणमादाय व्रजत्यूर्ध्वं सुषुम्नया ।
उद्घाटयेत्कपाटं तु यथा कुञ्चिकया हठात् ।।६७।।
कुण्डलिन्या तया योगी मोक्षद्वारं विभेदयेत् ।।६८।।

कृत्वा संपुटितौ करौ दृढतरं बद्धाथ पद्मासनं गाढं वक्षसि
सन्निधाय चुबुकं ध्यानं च तच्चेतसि ।
वारंवारमपातमूर्ध्वमनिलं प्रोच्चारयन्पूरितं मुञ्चन्प्राणमुपैति
बोधमतुलं शक्तिप्रभावान्नरः ।।६९।।

पद्मासनस्थितो योगी नाडीद्वारेषु पूरयन् ।
मारुतं कुम्भयन्यस्तु स मुक्तो नात्र संशयः ।।७०।।

अङ्गानां मर्दनं कृत्वा श्रमजातेन वारिणा ।
कट्वम्ललवणत्यागी क्षीरपानरतः सुखी ।।७१।।
ब्रह्मचारी मिताहारी योगी योगपरायणः ।
अब्दादूर्ध्वं भवेत्सिद्धो नात्र कार्या विचारणा ।।७२।।
कन्दोर्ध्वकुण्डली शक्तिः स योगी सिद्धिभाजनम् ।
अपानप्राणयोरैक्यं क्षयान्मूत्रपुरीषयोः ।।७३।।

युवा भवति वृध्दोऽपि सततं मूलबन्धनात् ।
पार्ष्णिभागेन संपीद्य योनिमाकुञ्चयेद्गुदम् ।।७४।।
अपानमूर्ध्वमुत्कृश्य मूलबन्धोऽयमुच्यते ।७५।

उड्यानं कुरुते यस्मादविश्रान्तमहाखगः ।।७५।।
उड्डियानं तदेव स्यात्तत्र बन्धो विधीयते ।
उदरे पश्चिमं ताणं नाभेरुर्ध्वं तु कारयेत् ।।७६।।
उड्डियानोऽप्ययं बन्धो मृत्युमतङ्गकेसरी ।
बध्नाति हि शिरोजातमधोगामिनभोजलम् ।।७७।।

ततो जालन्धरो बन्धः कर्मदुःखौघनाशनः ।
जालन्धरे कृते बन्धो कण्ठकोचलक्षणे ।।७८।।
न पीयूषं पतत्यग्नौ न च वायुः प्रधावति ।७९।

कपालकुहरे जिह्वा प्रविष्टा विपरीतगा ।।७९।।
भ्रुवोरन्तर्गता दृष्टिर्मुद्रा भवति खेचरी ।
न रोगो मरणं तस्य न निद्रा न क्षुधा तृषा ।।८०।।
न च मूर्च्छा भरेत्तस्य यो मुद्रां वेत्ति खेचरीम् ।

पीड्यते न च रोगेण लिप्यते न च कर्मणा ।।८१।।
बध्यते न च कालेन यस्य मुद्रास्ति खेचरी ।८२।

चित्तं चरति खे यस्माज्जिह्वा भवति खेगता ।।८२।।
तेनैषा खेचरी नाम मुद्रा सिद्धनमस्कृता
खेचर्या मुद्रया यस्य लम्बिकोर्ध्वतः ।।८३।।
बिन्दुः क्षरति नो यस्य कामिन्यालिङ्गितस्य च ।
यावद्बिन्दुः स्थितो देहे तावन्मृत्युभयं कुतः ।।८४।।
यावद्बद्धा नभोमुद्रा तावद्बिन्दुर्न गच्छति ।
गलितोऽपि यदा बिन्दुः संप्राप्तो योनिमण्डले ।।८५।।
व्रजत्यूर्ध्वं हठाच्छक्त्या निबद्धो योनिमुद्रया ।८६।

स एव द्विविधो बिन्दुः पाण्डरो लोहितस्तथा ।।८६।।
पाण्डरं शुक्रमित्याहुर्लोहिताख्यं महारजः ।
विद्रुमद्रुमसंकाशं योनिस्थाना स्थितं रजः ।।८७।।
शशिस्थाने वसेद्विन्दुस्तयोरैक्यं सुदुर्लभम् ।
बिन्दुः शिवो रजः शक्तिर्बिन्दुरिन्दु रजो रविः ।।८८।।
उभयोः संगमादेव प्राप्यते परमं वपुः ।
वायुना शक्तिचालेन प्रेरितं खे यथा रजः ।।८९।।
रविणैकत्वमायाति भवेद्दिव्यं वपुस्तदा ।
शुक्लं चन्द्रेण संयुक्तं रजः सूर्यसमन्वितं ।।९०।।
द्वयोः समरसीभावं यो जानाति स योगवित् ।९१।

शोधनं मलजालानां घटनं चन्द्रसूर्ययोः ।।९१।।
रसानां शोषणं सम्यङ्महामुद्राभिधीयते ।।९२।।

वक्षस्यस्तहनुर्निपीड्य सुषिरं योनेश्च वामाङ्घ्रिणा
हस्ताभ्यामनुधारयन्प्रविततं पादं तथा दक्षिणम् ।
आपूर्य श्वसनेन कुक्षियुगलं बध्वा शनै रेचयेदेषा पातकनाशिनी
ननु महामुद्रा नृणां प्रोच्यते ।।९३।।

अथात्मनिर्णयं व्याख्यास्ये ।।
हृदिस्थाने अष्टदलपद्मं वर्तते तन्मध्ये रेखावलयं कृत्वा
जीवात्मरूपं ज्योतीरूपमणुमात्रं वर्तते तस्मिन्सर्वं प्रतिष्ठितं
भवति सर्वं जानाति सर्वं करोति सर्वमेतच्चरितमहं कर्ता ऽहं
भोक्ता सुखी दुःखी काणः खञ्जो बधिरो मूकः कृशः स्थूलो
ऽनेन प्रकारेण स्वतन्त्रवादेन वर्तते ।।
पूर्वदले विश्रमते पूर्वं दलं श्वेतवर्णं तदा भक्तिपुरःसरं धर्मे
मतिर्भवति ।।
यदाऽग्नेयदले विश्रमते तदाग्नेयदलं रक्तवर्णं तदा
निद्रालस्यमतिर्भवति ।।
यदा दक्षिणदले विश्रमते तद्दक्षिणदलं कृष्णवर्णं तदा
द्वेषकोपमतिर्भवति ।।
यदा नैरृतदले विश्रमति तन्नैरृतदलं नीलवर्णं तदा
पापकर्महिंसामतिर्भवति ।।
यदा पश्चिमदले विश्रमते तत्पश्चिमदलं स्फटिकवर्णं तदा
क्रीडाविनोदे मतिर्भवति ।।
यदा वायव्यदले विश्रमते वायव्यदलं माणिक्यवर्णं तदा
गमनचलनवैरग्यमतिर्भवति ।।
यदुत्तरदले विश्रमते तदुत्तरदलं पीतवर्णं तदा
सुखशृङ्गारमतिर्भवति ।।

यदेशानदले विश्रमते तदीशनदलं वैडूर्यवर्णं तदा दानादिकृपामतिर्भवति ।।

यदा संधिसंधिषु मतिर्भवति तदा वातपित्तश्लेष्ममहाव्याधिप्रकोपो भवति ।।

यदा मध्ये तिष्ठति तदा सर्वं जानाति गायति नृत्यति पठत्यानन्दं करोति ।।

यदा नेत्रश्रमो भवति श्रमनिर्भरणार्थं प्रथमरेखाबन्धूकपुष्पवर्णं तदा निद्रावस्था भवति ।।

निद्रावस्थामध्ये स्वप्नावस्था भवति ।।

स्वप्नावस्थामध्ये दृष्टं श्रुतमनुमानसंभववार्ता इत्यादिकल्पनां करोति तदादिश्रमो भवति ।।

श्रमनिर्हरणार्थं द्वितीयरेखावलयं कृत्वा मध्ये निमज्जनं कुरुते द्वितीयरेखा इन्द्रकोपवर्णं तदा सुषुप्त्यवस्था भवति सुषुप्तौ केवलपरमेश्चरसंबन्धिनी बुद्धिर्भवति नित्यबोधस्वरूपा भवति पश्चात्परमेश्वरस्वरूपेण प्राप्तिर्भवति ।।

तृतीयरेखावलयं कृत्वा मध्ये निमज्जनं कुरुते तृतीयरेखा पद्मरागवर्णं तदा तुरीयावस्था भवति तुरीये केवलपरमात्मसंबन्धिनी भवति नित्यबोधस्वरूपा भवति तदा शनैः शनैरुपरमेद्बुद्ध्या धृतिगृहीतयात्मसंस्थं मनः कृत्वा न किंचिदपि चिन्तयेत्तदा प्राणापानयोरैक्यं कृत्वा सर्वं विश्वमात्मस्वरूपेण लक्ष्यं धारयति ।

यदा तुरीयातीतावस्था तदा सर्वेषामानन्दस्वरूपो भवति द्वन्द्वातीतो भवति यावद्देहधारणा वर्तते तावत्तिष्ठति पश्चात्परमात्मस्वरूपेण प्राप्तिर्भवति इत्यनेन प्रकारेण मोक्षो भवतीदमेवात्मदर्शनोपाया भवन्ति ।।

चतुष्पथसमायुक्तमहाद्वारकवायुना ।
सहस्थितत्रिकोणार्धगमने दृश्यते ऽच्युतः ।।९४।।

पूर्वोक्तत्रिकोणस्थानादुपरि पृथिव्यादिपञ्चवर्णकं ध्येयम् ।
प्राणादिपञ्चवायुश्च बीजं वर्णं च स्थानकम् ।
यकारं प्राणबीजं च नीलजीमूतसन्निभम् ।
रखारमग्निबीजं च अपानादित्यसंनिभम् ।।९५।।
लकारं पृथिवीरूपं व्यानं बन्धूकसंनिभम् ।
वकारं जीवबीजं च उदानं शङ्खवर्णकम् ।।९६।।
हकारं वियत्स्वरूपं च समानं स्फटिकप्रभम् ।९७।

हृन्नाभिनासाकर्णं च पादाङ्गुष्ठादिसंस्थितम् ।।९७।।
द्विसप्ततिसहस्राणि नाडीमार्गेषु वर्तते ।
अष्टाविंशतिकोटीषु रोमकूपेषु संस्थिताः ।।९८।।
समानप्राण एकस्तु जीवः स एक एव हि ।९९।

रेचकादि त्रयं कुर्याद्दृढचित्तः समाहितः ।।९९।।
शनैः समस्तमाकृष्य हृत्सरोरुहकोटरे ।
प्राणापानौ च बद्ध्वा तु प्रणवेन समुच्चरेत् ।।१००।।
कर्णसंकोचनं कृत्वा लिङ्गसंकोचनं तथा
मूलाधारात्सुषुम्ना च पद्मतन्तुनिभा सुभा ।।१०१।।
अमूर्तो वर्तते नादो वीणादण्डसमुत्थितः ।
शङ्खनादादिभिश्चैव मध्यमेव ध्वनिर्यथा ।।१०२।।
व्योमरन्ध्रगतो नादो मायूरं नादमेव च ।
कपालकुहरे मध्ये चतुर्द्वारस्य मध्यमे ।।१०३।।

तदात्मा राजते तत्र यथा व्योम्नि दिवाकरः ।
कोदण्डद्वयमध्ये तु ब्रह्मरन्ध्रेशक्त्या च ॥१०४॥
स्वात्मानं पुरुषं पश्येन्मनस्तत्र लयं गतम् ।
रत्नानि ज्योत्स्निनादं तु बिन्दुमाहेश्वरं पदम् ।
य एवं वेद पुरुषः स कैवल्यं समश्नुत इत्युपनिषत् ॥१०५॥

इति ध्यानबिन्दूपनिषत्समाप्ता ॥

2. Continuous Translation

Having meditated on the totality of Brahman, I reflect mentally on the remainder of my own totality, the fruit of knowledge, the essence of yoga, saying Om, may this [teaching] benefit both of us together. Peace.

1.
Even if sin extends [like] a mountain [for] many *yojanas*, it is destroyed by *dhyānayoga*; [there has] never [been] another destroyer.

2.
The *nāda* is above the *bīja akṣara*, the supreme point. That sound, when it disappears in the indestructible, [becomes] the soundless supreme seat.

3.
That yogin, in whom the highest sound of that sound is no more, has lost [all] doubt [that] the soundless sound [is] the highest [stage of *nāda yoga*].

4.
If the point [of] a hair is divided into one hundred thousand [parts], [and] if this *nāda* is divided into half of [each] division, then when this is absorbed, [the *yogin* attains] the pure [state].

5 to 7.
Just as fragrance [is] in flowers, ghee in milk, oil in sesame, gold in rocks, thus one who knows the Vedas is established in Brahman, having rejected sensual pleasure [and being of] stable mind, [sees] all creatures, like a string [of] pearls, in the self. So just as the oil is dependent on the sesame and fragrance on the flower, so does *puruṣa* exist in the body, [both] outside [and] inside.

8.
Now [the *yogin*] knows the tree with parts [and] its shadow without parts [and that] the Self exists everywhere, in the state with parts [and] without parts.

9a.
It is declared the one imperishable sound *Om* should be contemplated on as Brahman by all who desire liberation.

9b to 13a.
Pṛthivī, Agni, Rigveda, Bhūḥ and Brahma are absorbed when the sound 'A', the first part [of] *praṇava*, is attained. The region between heaven and earth, knowledge of sacrifice, air element, astral plane [and] Vishnu, harasser of men are [all] absorbed when the sound 'U', the second part [of] *praṇava*, is attained. The sky, sun, sounds [of] the Sāmaveda and even the Great Lord Śiva are [all] absorbed when the sound 'M', the third part [of] *praṇava*, is attained. The letter 'A' [is] yellow [in] colour [and] is said to be rajasic. The letter 'U' [is] white [and] sattvic. The letter 'M' [is] black [and] tamasic.

13b to 15.
He who does not know *Omkāra* [as having] eight parts, four feet, three states and five deities is not a Brahman. It is said thus: *praṇava* is the bow, *ātmā* the arrow, *brahma* the aim. Aiming carefully, he, like the arrow, becomes one with it. When the totality of this is seen, it reverses all actions.

16 to 19.
Deities [have] the power of *Oṃkāra*. Sounds [have] the power of *Oṃkāra*. All the three worlds [including] animals [and] plants [have] the power of *Oṃkāra*. The short [accent of Om] burns sins; the long one [is] imperishable [and] bestows good fortune. United with the half-syllable, *praṇava* [is] the giver [of] liberation. Like the uninterrupted flow [of]

oil [or] like the long sound [of] a bell, the end of *praṇava* [is] not to be uttered. Whoever knows this knows the true meaning of the Vedas. One should meditate on *Oṃkāra* [as] *Īśvara* [who] is like an unwavering light, the size of a thumb [and] motionless in the centre [of] the pericarp of the lotus [of] the heart.

20 to 25.

Inhaling *vāyu* through the left nostril, filling the whole stomach, one should meditate on *Oṃkāra* [as] being in the middle [of] the body, concealed [and] surrounded by flames. Brahmā is said to be inhalation; Viṣṇu is said to be breath retention; Rudra is said to be exhalation. [They are] the deities of *prāṇāyāma.* One can see [them], [although] concealed, through the practice of churning, [that is] *dhyāna*, by making the *ātman* the *arani* and *praṇava* the more powerful *arani.* By hearing the sound [of] *Oṃkāra* [and] restraining as much as possible both inhalation and exhalation, one should devote oneself to its form until one is completely absorbed in the inner sound. Those who see the lone *oṃkāra* [as] the form [of] *haṃsa* staying in all beings, shining [like] ten million suns, ever going and coming, devoid of movement, they become free from dust. That intelligence, which [is] the originator [of] creation, preservation [and] destruction in the three worlds, becomes absorbed [in the *Oṃkāra*]. That [is] the Supreme Seat of Viṣṇu.

26 to 29.

Now the lotus [of] the heart [has] eight petals [and] thirty-two staminae; the sun is in its centre; the moon has gone to the centre of the sun. *Agni* has gone to the centre of the moon; the spiritual light has gone to the centre of *Agni*. The seat, covered with many gems, is in the midst of the spiritual light. [One should hold] the stainless Vāsudeva in the centre [of] this seat, on his chest the black mark [and] celebrated jewel, adorned with gems and pearls, resembling pure crystal [and] as splendid as ten million moons. Thus one should meditate humbly on the great Viṣṇu.

30 to 35.
On inhalation one should meditate on the four-armed Mahā Viṣṇu resembling the *atasī* flower [and] situated in the area [of] the navel. On retention of breath, one should meditate in the area of the heart on the Grandfather Brahman with four faces [and] a reddish-yellow lustre, seated [on] a lotus. Then, on exhalation, for knowledge of the Self [one should meditate] at the eyebrow centre on the three-eyed Śiva, stainless, destroying all sins, resembling pure crystal; Śiva, the form of all the Vedas, like the flower of the plantain tree, its face down, stalk above, nourishing the leaf [and] the flower below, the pericarp [of the] lotus filled at a hundred angles with a hundred petals and others. There one should meditate upon the sun, the moon and Vahni up high. Having moved up through the lotus [whose] consciousness resembles the Sun, Agni [and] the Moon, [and] moistening [his] heart with it, he definitely reaches the Self.

36 and 37.
Whoever knows the three seats, the three mātras, the three Brahmas and the three akṣaras, or the three mātras [of] the half-mātra, he [has] the knowledge of the Vedas. Whoever knows [that that which] has surpassed *bindu*, nāda [and] *kalā* [is] uninterrupted like a stream [of] oil [and] as long as the sound [of] a bell, he [has] the knowledge of the Vedas.

38 to 40.
Just as a man draws up water through the hollow stalk [of] a lotus, so should the yogin, established on the path of yoga, draw in the breath. Having made the seed vessel [of] the lotus flower in the form of *ardhamātrā*, he should draw [the breath] through the stalk of the *mātrā*, [and] absorb [it] at the

eyebrow centre. He should know [that] the seat [of] nectar [is] the base of the nose as well as at the eyebrow centre in the forehead. This [is] the great abode [of] the Supreme Spirit.

41.
Postures, restraint of breath, withdrawal of the senses; concentration, meditation and self-realisation: these are the six limbs of yoga.

42 and 43a.
[There are] as many living creatures as [there are] postures, and the Great Lord recognises their incomparable differences. It is said [that] *siddha, bhadra,* as well as *simha* and *padma* [are] the four [main postures].

43b to 50a.
[The site of] the first chakra [is] the base [and] the second [is] *svādhiṣṭhāna.* Between these two is said [to be] the site of *yoni* in the form of *Kāma.* [There is] a four-petalled lotus in the site of the anus, called the base [cakra]. In the middle of it is said [to be] the yoni called Kāma, extolled by the *siddhas.* In the centre of the yoni stands the *liṅgam*, facing west [and] split at the top like a precious stone. Whoever knows [this is] a knower of yoga. A quadrangular figure, [in] the form [of] molten gold [and] flashing like streaks of lightning, [is] situated above agni [and] below the genital organ. Prāṇa, whose seat is Svādhiṣṭhāna, arises with its own sound. Thus the cakra Svādhiṣṭhāna is even referred to as the genital organ. That cakra [within] the orb of the navel, where the body [is] filled with air like jewels with a string, is called *Maṇipūra*, city of jewels. The *jīva*, governed by [its] pure [and] sinful [actions], spins about in [this] great cakra [of] twelve spokes as long as it does not experience [its] true state.

50b to 53.
Above the genital organ [and] below the navel is a knot like a

bird's egg. From there arise seventy-two thousand nāḍīs. Of these thousands of nāḍīs, seventy-two are recognised. Of these it is declared [there are] ten main ones [which] carry the prāṇas. The ten are said to be the triplicate iḍā, piṅgalā and suṣumnā, and gāndhārī, hastijihvā and pūṣā as well as yaśasvinī, alambusā, kuhūratra [and] śaṅkhinī.

54 to 58a.

Thus the cakra containing the nāḍīs should always be understood by the yogin. The three nāḍīs, iḍā, piṅgalā [and] suṣumnā, [whose] deities [are] the Moon, Sun [and] Agni, are said to carry the prāṇas continuously. Iḍā is on the left side, piṅgalā on the right and suṣumnā in the middle. They are known to be the flowing paths of prāṇa. *Prāṇa, Upāna, Samāna, Udāna* and then *Nāga, Kūrma, Kṛkaraka, Devadatta* and *Dhanaṃjaya*: the first five are called prāṇas, [and] the five beginning with Nāga [are called] *vāyavas*. These forms of life move along the thousands of nāḍīs.

58b to 61a.

Jīva, [being] dependent on prāṇa and apāna, spreads downwards [and] upwards. Because it fluctuates between the left and right paths, one cannot see [it]. Just as a ball bounces up, [after] being thrown down with the stick in one's hand, so the jīva, hurled about [by] prāṇa and apāna, cannot rest. Prāṇa draws [itself] from apāna, and apāna draws [itself] from prāṇa, it is said like a bird from a rope. Whoever knows this is a knower of yoga.

61b to 65a.

Jīva goes out with the sound Ha, [and] enters again with the sound Sa, thus always repeating that mantra *Haṃsa Haṃsa.* Jīva always repeats this mantra twenty-one thousand six hundred times day and night, *ajapā gāyatrī* by name, forever giving liberation to the yogin. A man is freed from sins simply by the thought of it. Neither in the past nor in the future [is there] a science equal to this, a *japa* equivalent to this [or] a virtuous act level with this.

65b to 68.
Parameśvarī sleeps, having covered with her mouth that door through which way leads to the untainted place of Brahma. [Then] awakened by the union of agni with manas [and] prāṇa, having taken a needle-like quality, she passes upwards through suṣumnā. Just as with a key, the yogin should open [this] door with full force [and] split the door to liberation by means of the kuṇḍalinī.

69.
Folding the hands firmly, then fixed in *padmāsana,* placing the chin firmly on the chest and *dhyāna* on the mind, [one should] repeatedly raise the vital air upwards, inhale forcefully, and then release the prāṇa. A man [obtains] unequalled wisdom through [this] splendid *śakti.*

70.
The yogin who, seated in padmāsana, inhales [and] restrains the breath at the doors of the nāḍīs, is without doubt liberated here.

71 to 73.
Having wiped from the limbs the sweat produced by fatigue, forgoing [food which is] pungent [and] causes one to salivate, the yogin [who is] wholly devoted to yoga, loves to drink milk, [is] celibate [and] eats moderately, becomes a *siddha* in just over a year. No investigation needs to be done in this respect. [When] kuṇḍalinī śakti [is] up in the throat, [then] apāna [and] prāṇa are united, ending [the production of] urine [and] faeces, [and] the yogin receives siddhis.

74 and 75a.
Even an old person becomes young through constant mūlabandha. Pressing the yoni with part [of] the heel, one

should contract the anus, while raising the apāna upwards: this is called mūlabandha.

75b to 77.
Just like the great bird [which] flies upwards unwearied, such is *uddiyāna.* Therefore it is considered a *bandha.* One should put the western area of the stomach above the navel. This *uddiyāna bandha* [is] a lion [to] the elephant [of] death, since it binds the water [which], produced in the head, flows down.

78 and 79a.
In that way *jālandhara bandha* destroys the suffering of a multitude of karmas. When jālandhara bandha is performed, indicated by contraction of the throat, nectar does not fall in the fire, nor does the *vāyu* spread.

79b to 82a.
When the tongue, inverted, enters the cave of the skull, there is *khecarī,* the mudrā of sight concealed in the eyebrow [centre]. Whoever knows about this khecarī mudrā has neither sickness, nor death, nor sleep, nor hunger [or] thirst, nor fainting. Whoever does khecarī mudrā is neither afflicted by disease nor bound to *karma*, nor constrained by time.

82b to 86a.
Because the mind moves in space [and] the tongue has entered [this] space, therefore this mudrā of the name khecarī is worshipped by the seers. When the uvula [is pushed] upwards by khecarī mudrā, the bindu does not flow down, even when in the embrace [of] a lovely woman. Where is the fear [of] death, as long as the bindu stays in the body? As long as khecarī mudrā is held, then the bindu does not leave. Even when the bindu arrives at the ring of the yoni, contained there, it travels upwards through the forceful effort of yoni mudrā.

86b to 91a.

So this bindu [is] of two kinds, white [and] red. The white one is thus called *śukra* [and] the red is said [to have] much *rajas*. The rajas located in the area of the yoni looks like a column of coral. The bindu remains in the seat of the moon. The union of these two [is] very rare. The highest form can be reached through the coming together of these two: the Śiva energy [of] bindu [which is] the sun [and] the Śakti energy of bindu [which is] the moon. When rajas is directed heavenwards by the movement of the power of vāyu, then the body, approaching the unity [of] the sun's eclipse, becomes divine. *Śukla* is united with the moon; rajas is connected with the sun: whoever understands the merging of the two, that person is a knower of yoga.

91b to 93.

The cleansing of waste matter, the union of the moon with the sun, the drying of fluids, [this] is called the true mahā mudrā. Pressing the jaw down on the chest, and the hollow of the yoni with the left foot, then holding with both hands the stretched out right leg, having filled the whole abdomen with the breath, one should slowly exhale. This [is] indeed the mahā mudrā, said to destroy the sins of men.

94.

Now I shall describe in detail the atman. In the seat of the heart is a lotus [with] eight petals. In its centre abides the *jīvātman* in the form of a bright light, atomic in size [and] shaped as a circle. In it is placed everything. It knows everything. It does everything. It behaves thus: I am the doer. I am the enjoyer. [I am] happy, sad, one-eyed, lame, deaf, mute, thin, stout. In this way it exists independently.

[When] it rests on the eastern petal [which is] white [in] colour, then it is inclined to righteousness together with devotion. When it rests on the south-eastern petal [which is]

red [in] colour, then it is inclined to sleep [and] sloth. When it rests on the southern petal [which is] black [in] colour, then it is prone to hatred [and] anger. When it rests on the south-western petal [which is] blue [in] colour, then it is prone to sinful [and] violent actions. When it rests on the western petal [which is of] a crystal colour, then it is inclined to play [and] entertainment. When it rests on the north-western petal [which is of] a ruby colour, then it is inclined to walking, wandering [and] detachment. Whenever it rests on the northern petal [which is] yellow [in] colour, then its mind is happy [and] loving. When it rests on the north-eastern petal [which is] a deep, celestial blue, then it is inclined to compassion [and] donations etc. When it settles on the junctures [of the petals], then there is severe
disease [due to] an excess of wind, bile [or] phlegm. When it stays in the middle, then it knows everything, sings, dances, recites [and] is blissful. When the eye is in pain, in order to remove the pain [it makes] first an outline the colour [of] the bandhuka flower, then goes into the state of sleep. In the middle of the sleeping state is the dreaming state. In the midst of the dreaming state it creates the ideas relating to perception, memory, possibility, words and so on. Then there is pain etc. In order to have the pain removed, having made a second circular line, it sinks in the middle. The second circle is the colour of the insect Indragopa.

In deep sleep there is one thought [which] relates to the Supreme Being alone. [This state] has the quality [of] eternal wisdom, [which] it attains later through the nature [of] the Supreme Being. Having made a third circular line, it sinks in the middle. The third circle [is] a ruby colour. Then comes the fourth state. In the fourth state there is connection with the Supreme Spirit alone, becoming the nature of eternal wisdom. Then one should gradually await [the intuition] of *buddhi* with constancy and resolution. Having contained the mind [in] the ātman, one should think of nothing else. Having united prāṇa and apāna, one focuses one's aim on the whole universe through the nature of the atman. When [one is in] the state beyond the fourth, then one experiences everything [as] bliss [and] is beyond duality. One stays there as long as there is wearing of the body. Next one attains the nature [of] the Supreme Spirit. Through this means there is liberation. The approaches to knowing the ātman are surely this.

The Imperishable One is seen through the breath, entering the great hole [where] four paths meet, [and] the half triangle [which] abide together.

95 to 97a.
Above the area [of] the aforesaid triangle, one should meditate on the five letters [of] earth and the other [elements], the five vital airs [of] prāṇa etc, and the colour and position [of their] seeds. The letter ya [is] the seed of prāṇa, and resembles a blue cloud. The letter ra [is] the seed of agni, [is of the vital air] apāna, and resembles the sun. The letter la, the form of *pṛthivi*, [is of] vyāna, resembling the bandhuka flower. The letter va [is] the seed of jīva [of] udāna, and the colour of a conch. The letter ha [is] the form of *ākāśa*, [of] samāna, and [has] the radiance of crystal.

97b to 99a.
[The vital energies] located in the heart, navel, nose, ears, feet and fingers etc flow in the seventy-two thousand nāḍīs, are in the two hundred and eighty million hair-pores, [and] yet [is] one and the same energy. This [is] indeed the one jīva.

99b to 105.
[With] a strong [and] concentrated mind, one should do the three: exhalation etc. Slowly drawing in the whole [breath] and contracting the throat [and] genital organ, joining together prāṇa and apāna in the cave [of] the lotus [of] the

heart, one should chant the praṇava. From mūlādhāra is suṣumnā, resembling the radiant thread [of] the lotus. The subtle nāda rises up the spinal column, and its sound [from] the middle [is] like [that] of a conch etc. [When] it enters the opening [of] the ether, the sound is that of a peacock. In the middle [of] the cavity [of] the skull between the four doors, shines the ātman, just like the sun in the sky. Then between the two bows in the fontanelle, one sees puruṣa with śakti [as] one's own ātman. There the individual mind becomes absorbed. That person attains final liberation who understands gems, moonlight, nāda, bindu [and] the seat of Maheśvara. Thus speaks the Upaniṣad.

Thus concludes the Dhyānabindu Upaniṣad.

ABOUT THE AUTHOR

Swami Satyadharma was a senior sannyasin, a yoga acharya, and a versatile teacher of yogic meditation and allied philosophies, having a Master of Arts in Yoga Philosophy with First Class Honors from Bihar Yoga Bharati, India. She wrote the commentary on the *Yoga Chudamani Upanishad*, while living in India, which was published by Yoga Publications Trust in 2003. In 2015 she published her commentary on *Yoga Tattwa Upanishad,* in 2018 her commentary on *Yoga Darshan Upanishad*, and in March 2019 her commentary on *Yoga Kundali Upanishad.*

Born in Connecticut USA, she lived in India for over 35 years under the direct tutelage of her yoga master, Swami Satyananda Saraswati, where she imbibed the traditional yogic teachings, and became Director of the Department of Undergraduate Studies at Bihar Yoga Bharati. She has compiled and edited many major yoga publications, such as *Yoga Darshan, Sannyasa Darshan, Dharana Darshan* and the *Teachings of Swami Satyananda.* Her final years were spent in Australia, where she brought to light the ancient teachings of yoga in the form of the Yoga Upanishads.

ABOUT THE TRANSLATOR

Srimukti (Ruth Perini) was for many years a teacher of yoga and meditation. Already a linguist, having graduated in French, Italian and Japanese from the Universities of Sydney and Queensland, Australia, she undertook four years of studies in Sanskrit at the Australian National University (ANU) with Dr McComas Taylor. She was invited to join the Golden Key International Society for outstanding academic achievement, as she was awarded High Distinctions throughout her Sanskrit studies. She is the translator of *Yoga Tattwa Upanishad, Yoga Darshana Upanishad*, and *Yoga Kundali Upanishad,* commentaries by Swami Satyadharma.

Ruth (Srimukti) may be contacted on yoga.upanishads@yahoo.com.

www.ingramcontent.com/pod-product-compliance
Lightning Source LLC
Chambersburg PA
CBHW070253010526
44107CB00056B/2448
* 9 7 8 0 6 4 8 9 1 0 7 4 9 *